SINGER

SEWING REFERENCE LIBRARY®

Sewing Projects for the Home

Cy DeCosse Incorporated
Minnetonka, Minnesota

Sewing Projects
for the Home

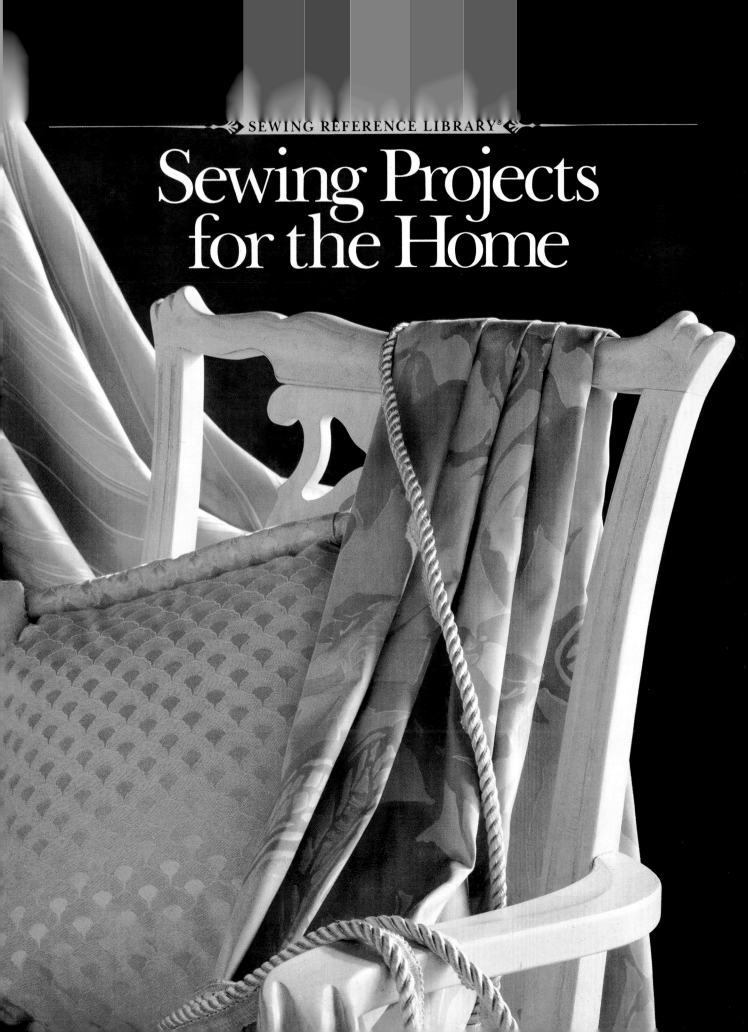

Contents

Copyright © 1991
Cy DeCosse Incorporated
5900 Green Oak Drive
Minnetonka, Minnesota 55343
1-800-328-3895
All rights reserved
Printed in U.S.A.

Also available from the publisher:
*Sewing Essentials, Sewing for the Home,
Clothing Care & Repair, Sewing for
Style, Sewing Specialty Fabrics, Sewing
Activewear, The Perfect Fit, Timesaving
Sewing, More Sewing for the Home,
Tailoring, Sewing for Children, Sewing
with an Overlock, 101 Sewing Secrets,
Sewing Pants That Fit, Quilting by
Machine, Decorative Machine Stitching,
Creative Sewing Ideas, Sewing Lingerie,*
*Sewing with Knits, More Creative
Sewing Ideas, Quilt Projects by Machine*

Library of Congress
Cataloging-in-Publication Data

Sewing projects for the home.

p. cm. — (Singer sewing reference
library)
Includes index.
ISBN 0-86573-262-0
ISBN 0-86573-263-9 (pbk.)
1. House furnishings. 2. Sewing.
I. Cy DeCosse Incorporated. II. Series.
TT387.S49 1991
646.2'1— dc20   91-4680

Distributed by: Contemporary Books, Inc.
  Chicago, Illinois

CY DECOSSE INCORPORATED
Chairman: Cy DeCosse
President: James B. Maus
Executive Vice President: William B. Jones

SEWING PROJECTS FOR THE HOME
Created by: The Editors of Cy DeCosse
  Incorporated, in cooperation with the
  Sewing Education Department, Singer
  Sewing Company. Singer is a trademark
  of The Singer Company and is used
  under license.

Executive Editor: Zoe A. Graul
Technical Director: Rita C. Opseth
Project Manager: Linda Halls
Senior Art Director: Lisa Rosenthal
Art Director: Yelena Konrardy
Writer: Rita C. Opseth
Editors: Janice Cauley, Bernice Maehren
Sample Coordinator: Carol Olson
Technical Photo Director: Bridget Haugh
Fabric Editor: Joanne Wawra
Sewing Staff: Phyllis Galbraith, Bridget
  Haugh, Sara Holmen, Linda Neubauer,
  Carol Olson, Lori Ritter, Nancy
  Sundeen
*Director of Development, Planning
  & Production:* Jim Bindas
Photo Studio Manager: Rebecca Boyle

Photographers: Phil Aarrestad, Rebecca
  Hawthorne, Rex Irmen, John Lauenstein,
  Bill Lindner, Mark Macemon, Charles
  Nields, Mette Nielsen, Mike Parker,
  Cathleen Shannon
Production Manager: Amelia Merz
Electronic Publishing Analyst:
  Kevin D. Frakes
Production Staff: Joe Fahey, Melissa
  Grabanski, Jim Huntley, Mark
  Jacobson, Duane John, Daniel Meyers,
  Linda Schloegel, Greg Wallace, Nik
  Wogstad
Consultants: JoAnn Brezette, Stephanie
  Carter, Kathy Ellingson, Amy Engman,
  Ann Fatigati, Pamela Hastings, Pam
  Marie, Dorothy Collins Shepherd

Contributors: Andersen Windows, Inc.;
  Calico Corners Decorative Fabrics;
  The Claesson Company, Inc.; Coats &
  Clark Inc.; Conso Products Company;
  Creative Home Textiles/Mill Creek;
  Gosling Tapes; Graber Industries, Inc.;
  Kirsch; Scandia Down Shops; Spartex
  Inc.; Swiss-Metrosene, Inc.; Textilis;
  Waverly, Division of F. Schumacher
  & Company

Printed on American paper by: Ringier
  America, Inc. (0293)

What You Will Learn

Slipcovers, pages 105 to 125.

Whether you want to redecorate your entire house, or just sew a few quick room accessories, *Sewing Projects for the Home* offers inspiration as well as step-by-step instructions.

In the Getting Started section, you will find tips for planning your project, including how to coordinate fabrics for an appealing room decor. Learn how to measure windows for curtains and valances and how to measure the bed for a duvet cover and bed skirt. This section also helps you calculate yardage, select fabrics, and sew seams for perfectly matched patterned fabrics.

In the Window Treatments section, we will show you how to make a variety of new window fashions and give you complete hardware information and installation instructions. For a tailored window treatment, try either the stagecoach or handkerchief valance. Or for a more feminine, ruffled look, sew a butterfly swag valance. If you like the look of swags, select from scarf swags with fabric rosettes, pole swags

Bed coverings, pages 87 to 101.

with fabric-covered drapery poles and finials, or rod-pocket swags and cascades. For the popular arch, or Palladian, window, sew a sheer sunburst curtain.

Choose from a wide selection of ideas in the Pillows section, including knotted-corner pillows, rosette pillows, and rolled bolsters. Learn how to make and apply different types of welting and how to sew a zippered pillow cover. We also give you tips for stuffing pillows.

Sewing for the Bedroom includes new styles for duvet covers, bed skirts, and pillow shams. Try either the circular ruffle bed skirt or the more elaborate swag bed skirt. Sew a duvet cover with jumbo welting or gathered welting; then make coordinated envelope pillow shams.

Slipcovers can update upholstered furniture. The Slipcovers section includes the basic techniques for pin-fitting a muslin pattern, cutting the fabric, sewing the slipcover, and making the cushions.

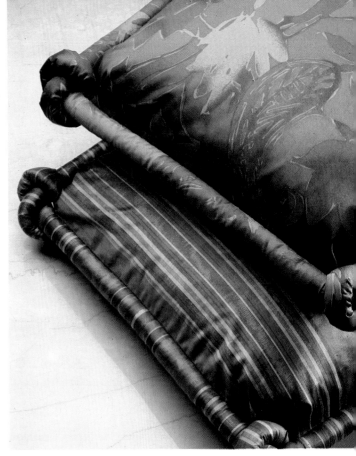

Pillows, pages 61 to 85.

Window treatments, pages 25 to 59.

PS-15

PL-14

PL-15

PS-15

Getting Started

Planning Your Project

The first step in planning any project, no matter how large or small, is to analyze the room in which the project will be placed. Think about what you like in the room and what you want to change. If possible, collect samples of any carpeting, fabric, wallpaper, or paint that will remain in the room. Then bring the samples with you to the fabric store, to help you coordinate the old and the new.

You may want to look through recent decorating magazines for ideas to inspire you in updating your room. Pictures can help you decide on a style you like. Rooms with several print fabrics tend to appear cozier and smaller. Rooms with mostly solid colors tend to look restful and larger. The colors you select can also have an effect on the way you feel. Bright, strong colors are more cheerful; muted colors, more relaxing.

Keep in mind that there is no right or wrong way to coordinate the decor of a room. Some general guidelines can help you make good decisions, but your own feelings and preferences are the most important consideration. Salespeople or designers may give helpful suggestions, but be sure to follow your own instincts if you are not comfortable with their ideas.

Learn about the various types of decorating fabrics that are available (pages 16 and 17). Bring home samples of the fabrics you are considering before making your final decisions. Place the samples where they will be used in the room. If a fabric will be used for a valance, place it at the top of the window. Be sure to check the fabrics during daytime and evening hours, since natural and artificial light affect the way colors match or coordinate. Leave the samples in place for a few days to be sure you are comfortable with your decisions. Your initial reactions may change.

Planning the Colors & Patterns

How to Plan a Coordinated Decor

When planning the style of a room, try to visualize the colors and patterns of your sewing projects and how they will be used in the room. Avoid using equal amounts of all the fabrics. Use the primary fabric for about two-thirds of the room furnishings, use a secondary fabric for about one-third, and use accent colors in small amounts. The size of the fabric samples should be in proportion to how they will be used, such as large samples for draperies, small samples for accent pillows.

Vary the textures in the room. Nubby or textured fabrics and surfaces, mixed with smooth ones, add interest. For example, textured sheers contrast with a shiny brass pole.

1) Select the primary patterned fabric. This will be the main fabric and will be used for about two-thirds of the fabric in the room. Select a print that will coordinate with existing furnishings, such as carpeting.

2) Add a secondary patterned fabric that includes some of the colors from the primary fabric. The secondary pattern is used for about one-third of the fabric in the room. Striped fabric works well as a secondary pattern, but florals or plaids may be used, if desired. Vary the scale of the pattern so it is different from the primary print.

3) Add accent patterned fabrics to be used in small amounts. These fabrics can introduce another color from the primary fabric. Or you can add texture by selecting fabrics such as lace; some prints have a textural appearance, even though the fabric has a smooth surface.

4) Select solid-colored fabrics to unify the patterned fabrics and give visual relief. Choose colors you want to emphasize from the other fabrics.

Mixing Patterned Fabrics

Plaid fabric was selected as the primary pattern, because a tailored style was desired. A traditional paisley print was chosen as the secondary pattern to soften the look and repeat the colors in the plaid. The striped fabric adds a bright accent.

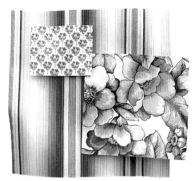

Floral patterns are traditionally the basis for a romantic look. A coordinated fabric group designed by the manufacturer was used for this decorating scheme. The soft colors of the prints are accented with a brighter solid color.

Geometric designs give a more active, contemporary look. These patterned fabrics have a rich textural appearance and an interesting mix of color. The solid-colored accent fabric emphasizes one of the colors in the prints, while its ribbed texture contrasts with the smooth finish of the patterned fabrics.

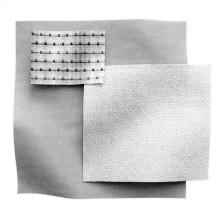

Solid-colored fabrics were selected as the primary and secondary fabrics, giving a more passive look to the room. The colors are compatible, yet offer contrast. Texture has been used to provide variety. For an accent fabric, a novelty weave was used to tie in the colors of the solid fabrics.

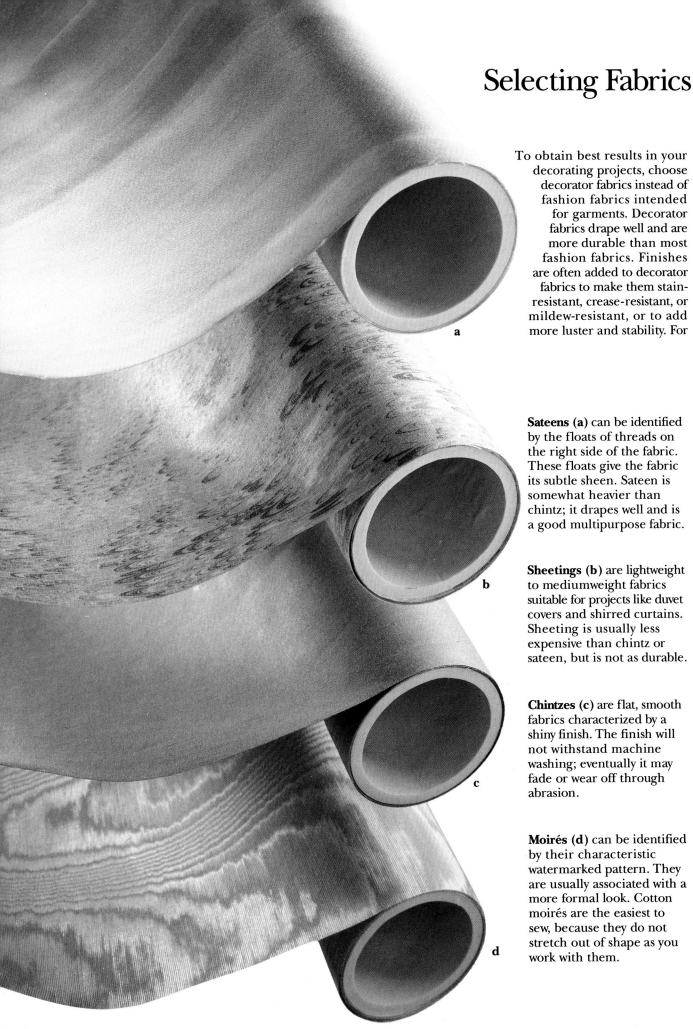

Selecting Fabrics

To obtain best results in your decorating projects, choose decorator fabrics instead of fashion fabrics intended for garments. Decorator fabrics drape well and are more durable than most fashion fabrics. Finishes are often added to decorator fabrics to make them stain-resistant, crease-resistant, or mildew-resistant, or to add more luster and stability. For

Sateens (a) can be identified by the floats of threads on the right side of the fabric. These floats give the fabric its subtle sheen. Sateen is somewhat heavier than chintz; it drapes well and is a good multipurpose fabric.

Sheetings (b) are lightweight to mediumweight fabrics suitable for projects like duvet covers and shirred curtains. Sheeting is usually less expensive than chintz or sateen, but is not as durable.

Chintzes (c) are flat, smooth fabrics characterized by a shiny finish. The finish will not withstand machine washing; eventually it may fade or wear off through abrasion.

Moirés (d) can be identified by their characteristic watermarked pattern. They are usually associated with a more formal look. Cotton moirés are the easiest to sew, because they do not stretch out of shape as you work with them.

best results, do not preshrink decorator fabrics. Washing may remove the finishes, change the fabric's hand, or fade the colors. Dry cleaning is recommended to keep the finished projects looking their best. Several types of fabric may be used in one room. When different fabric types are used, the various surface textures add interest and variety to the decor.

Sheers (a) are lightweight fabrics that add softness to a window treatment and allow light to filter into the room for a bright, airy look. They usually have plain weaves or linenlike textures.

Laces (b), available in many patterns and weights, add texture to the room decor. When used at the window, lace lets in light. Lace may also be used for room accessories, such as tablecloths and pillows.

Duck (c) and lightweight canvas are coarsely woven and have a flat finish. Medium to heavy in weight, they are durable fabrics suitable for casual decorating.

Novelty weaves (d) have woven-in patterns or designs. They add texture and interest to the decor of a room.

Finished width of window treatment or length of rod or mounting board

Outside frame

Inside frame

Length of window to sill

Length of window to apron

Measuring Windows

Before measuring the windows, select the style of the window treatment and the hardware. Decide where the window treatment will be positioned and install the hardware, so accurate measurements can be taken.

Hardware, including curtain rods, swag holders, and mounting boards, can be mounted inside or outside the window frame. For an inside mount, install the hardware inside the top of the window frame so the molding is exposed. For an outside mount, install the hardware at the top of the window frame or on the wall above the window. When the hardware is mounted above the window frame, visual height is added to the window treatment. Cascades and side treatments can be mounted so they cover part of the wall at the sides of the window, adding visual width. When window treatments are mounted onto the wall, more glass can be exposed, letting in more light.

Draperies can be either sill-length, apron-length, or floor-length. For good proportion, valances and swags are often one-fifth the length of the window

or the completed window treatment. Cascades are often one-third or two-thirds the length of the window. Avoid dividing the window treatment in half visually.

To determine the finished length of the window treatment, measure from the top of the curtain rod or mounting board to the desired length of the window treatment; if the window treatment will have a heading above the rod, add the length of the heading to this measurement. To determine the finished width, measure the length of the drapery rod. For some window treatments, it may also be necessary to measure the width of the return, or the distance that the rod projects out from the wall.

Use a folding ruler or metal tape measure for taking accurate measurements; cloth or vinyl tape measures may stretch or sag. If you are making window treatments for several windows in the same room, measure and record the measurements for each window separately, even if they appear to be the same size.

Measuring Beds

When measuring a bed for a duvet or comforter, measure the bed over the blankets and sheets that will normally be used. The measurements will be larger than the mattress size, but this ensures that the bed covering will fit correctly. Measure the width of the bed from side to side across the top, and measure the length from the head of the bed to the foot.

Duvets or comforters reach 1" to 4" (2.5 to 10 cm) below the mattress on the sides and at the foot of

the bed. Determine the drop length of the duvet or comforter by measuring the distance from the top of the bed to the desired position for the lower edge of the duvet. The drop length is usually 9" to 12" (23 to 30.5 cm), depending on the mattress depth.

When measuring for a bed skirt, measure from the top of the box spring to the floor; then subtract ½" (1.3 cm) for clearance.

Drop length of duvet

Drop length of bed skirt

Estimating Yardage

Because fabric widths vary, the yardage requirements for decorating projects cannot be calculated until the fabric has been selected. After you have taken the necessary measurements and determined the finished size of the project, you will need to figure the cut length and cut width of the project.

To determine the cut length and cut width of a fabric that does not require matching, add the amounts needed for any hems, rod pockets, headings, ease, seam allowances, and fullness to the finished size of the project. For example, if you are sewing a gathered valance, add the amount needed for rod pockets, headings, and hems to the finished length; then add side hems, seam allowances, and fullness to the finished width. If the fabric requires matching, you will need to allow extra fabric (page 22). Each project in this book includes the instructions for determining the cut length and cut width of the fabric.

Frequently a decorating project will require more than one width of fabric. To determine the number of fabric widths required, divide the cut width of the project by the width of the fabric.

To calculate the amount of fabric you will need, multiply the cut length of the project by the number of fabric widths required; this is the total fabric length in inches (centimeters). Divide this measurement by 36" (100 cm) to determine the number of yards (meters) required.

Rod-sleeve valance (page 38) is made from striped fabric that has been railroaded, changing the direction of the stripes. The stripes run on the lengthwise grain on the fabric, but are turned horizontally on the railroaded valance. The curtains were not railroaded, so the lengthwise grain of the fabric runs lengthwise on the curtain.

Railroading Fabrics

Many fabrics can be railroaded, or cut so the lengthwise grain will run horizontally on the finished project. This is possible when the cut length is shorter than the fabric width. Railroading is often used for cutting fabric for valances, bed skirts, and short curtains to eliminate seams and save sewing time.

If the fabric is patterned, check to see that the design can be turned sideways. Flowers with stems, birds, and other one-way designs cannot be turned sideways. Striped fabrics may be railroaded, but stripes on the lengthwise grain will run horizontally if the fabric is railroaded.

Yardage requirements are calculated differently when fabric is railroaded. To determine how many yards (meters) of fabric you will need, divide the cut width by 36" (100 cm). Depending on the project, railroading may require more or less fabric.

Sunburst curtain (page 42) has been railroaded to prevent seams. Seams would be noticeable in the sheer fabric when light comes through the window.

Handkerchief valance (page 36) has been railroaded to prevent seams, which would detract from the overall appearance of the valance.

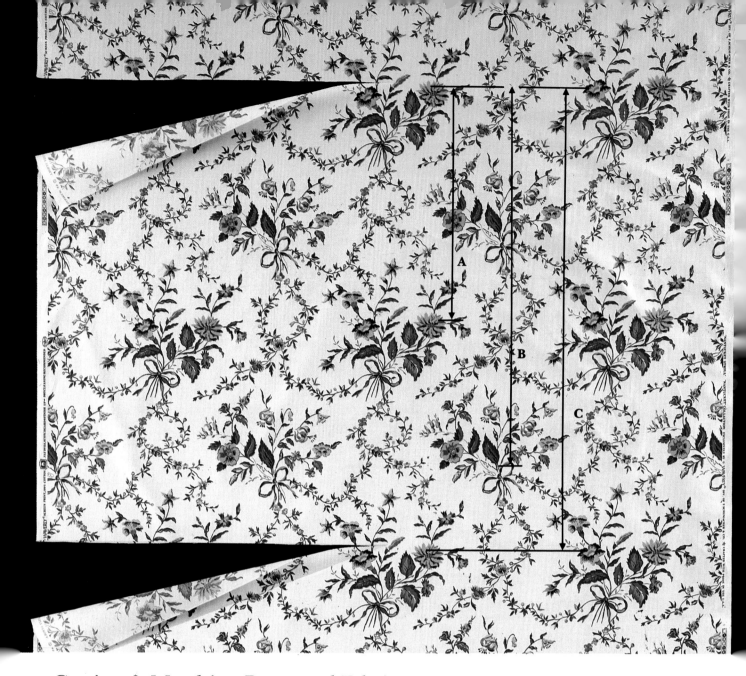

Cutting & Matching Patterned Fabrics

For professional results, always match the pattern of a fabric at the seamlines. Extra yardage is usually needed in order to match the pattern.

The pattern repeat (A) is the lengthwise distance from one distinctive point on the pattern, such as the tip of a particular petal in a floral pattern, to the same point in the next pattern design. Some patterned fabrics have pattern repeat markings (+) printed on the selvage. These markings mark the beginning of each pattern repeat, and they are especially helpful for fabrics that include several similar designs.

Add the amounts needed for any hems, rod pockets, headings, ease, seam allowances, and fullness to the finished length, to determine how long the lengths of fabric need to be (B). Then round this measurement up to the next number divisible by the size of the pattern repeat. This is the cut length (C). For example, if the pattern repeat (A) is 19" (48.5 cm), and the finished length plus hems, rod pockets, and other allowances (B) is 30" (76 cm), the actual cut length (C) is 38" (96.5 cm). To have patterns match from one panel to the next, each panel must be cut at the same point on the pattern repeat.

To calculate the amount of fabric you will need, multiply the cut length by the number of fabric widths required for the project; add one additional pattern repeat so you can adjust the placement of the pattern on the cut lengths. This is the total fabric length in inches (centimeters); divide this measurement by 36" (100 cm) to determine the number of yards (meters) required.

How to Match a Patterned Fabric

1) Position the fabric widths, right sides together, matching the selvages.

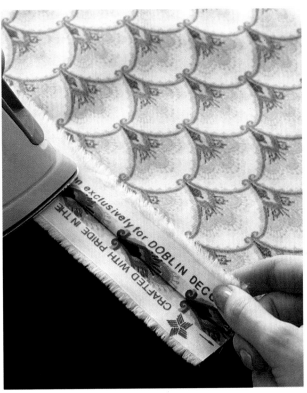

2) Fold selvage back at one end until pattern matches. Lightly press foldline.

3) Unfold selvage. Pin on foldline; check the match from right side.

4) Reposition pins perpendicular to foldline; stitch on foldline. Trim away selvages. Trim fabric to finished length plus hems, rod pockets, and other allowances, as calculated opposite.

Window Treatments

Drapery Hardware

Select the drapery hardware before measuring for the window treatment, because the cut length of the fabric will vary, depending on the drapery rods.

Support drapery rods with brackets to prevent the rods from bowing in the middle. The brackets are usually positioned at intervals of 45" (115 cm) or less, across the width of the window. Whenever possible, screw the brackets into wall studs. Use molly bolts if it is necessary to install brackets between wall studs into drywall or plaster.

How to Install a Drapery Rod Bracket Between Wall Studs Using Molly Bolts

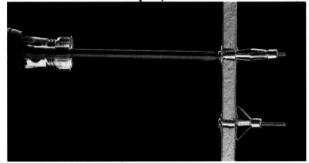

1) Hold drapery rod bracket at desired placement; mark hole locations. Drill 5/16" (7.5 mm) holes into drywall or plaster; for heavy window treatments, use two molly bolts for each bracket. Tap long molly bolt into drilled hole. Tighten screw; molly bolt expands as it is tightened.

2) Remove screw from molly bolt; insert screw into drapery rod bracket. Align screw to installed molly bolt. Screw bracket securely in place.

Basic Rods

Curtain rods **(a)** are used for simple rod-pocket curtains and valances. When lace or sheer fabric is used, select a curtain rod of clear or opaque plastic to prevent it from showing through and detracting from the fabric.

Wide curtain rods **(b),** known as Continental® and Dauphine™ rods, available in both 2½" (6.5 cm) and 4½" (11.5 cm) widths, add depth and interest to the rod pockets of shirred curtains and top treatments. Corner connectors are used to make these rods suitable for bay windows and corner windows. The connectors allow you to sew a continuous window treatment, without interruptions or breaks in the treatment at the corners.

Flexible ⅜" (1 cm) plastic tubing **(c)**, found in the plumbing department of hardware stores, can be shaped to fit the curve of arch windows.

Decorative Pole Sets

Contemporary metal pole sets **(d)**, or Cirmosa® pole sets, can be used for multiple-rod treatments, such as the rod-sleeve valances on page 38. These drapery rods, also available for traverse draperies, have metallic and pearlized finishes in several colors.

Traditional brass pole sets **(e)** come in various sizes and finial styles. Brass hardware is used for rod-pocket curtains and valances as well as with draped swags or pole swags. Brass rods in smaller diameters can be bent for use in bay windows.

Wood pole sets **(f)** with plain or fluted poles are available in finished or unfinished wood. Finials in various styles give the wood poles a decorator look. The poles and finials may be covered with fabric, or painted.

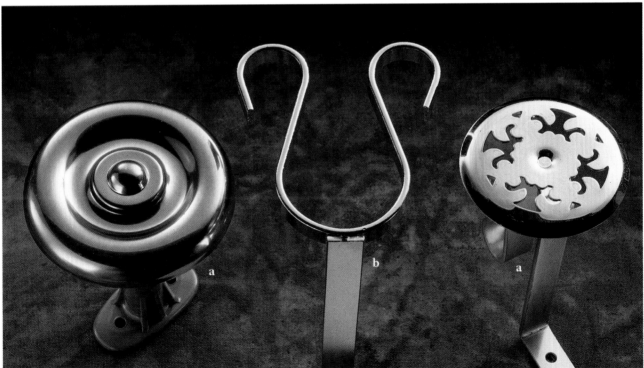

Drapery accessories are used to secure the draped fabric in swag window treatments and in tieback draperies. Tieback holders **(a)** with projection arms or stems are used instead of fabric tiebacks to hold curtains in place. They may also be used for scarf swag window treatments (page 44). Swag holders **(b)** are also used for scarf swags when rosettes are desired.

Covering & Installing Mounting Boards

Some window treatments are mounted on boards instead of being hung on drapery rods. For a professional look, cover the mounting board with fabric. This gives it a more finished appearance and protects the window treatment from being snagged by unfinished wood.

The mounting board is cut to the finished width of the window treatment and may be mounted inside or outside the window frame. For an inside mount, the board is attached inside the window frame, using #8 gauge 1½" (3.8 cm) pan-head screws. Predrill the holes for the screws, using a ⅛" (3 mm) drill bit.

For an outside mount, the board is installed at the top of the window frame or on the wall above the window. For clearance, the board is cut wider than the outside measurement of the window frame or undertreatment, and it projects out from the wall farther than the window frame or undertreatment. Angle irons are used to install the mounting board. The angle irons must be a little shorter than the width of the mounting board. Whenever possible, screw the angle irons into wall studs, using pan-head screws and predrilling the holes for the screws, using a ⅛" (3 mm) drill bit. If it is necessary to install angle irons between wall studs into drywall or plaster, use molly bolts to ensure a secure installation. To prevent the mounting board from bowing in the middle, position angle irons at 45" (115 cm) intervals or less.

Supplies include mounting board **(a)**, angle irons **(b)**, pan-head screws **(c)**, and molly bolts **(d)**.

How to Determine the Size of the Mounting Board

Inside mount. Cut 1" × 1" (2.5 × 2.5 cm) mounting board ½" (1.3 cm) shorter than inside measurement of window frame, to ensure that the board will fit inside the frame after it is covered with fabric.

Outside mount. Cut mounting board 2" (5 cm) longer than width of undertreatment or window frame and at least 2" (5 cm) wider than projection of undertreatment or window frame.

How to Cover the Mounting Board with Fabric

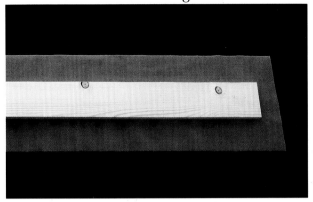

1) Cut fabric to cover mounting board, with width of fabric equal to distance around board plus 1" (2.5 cm) and length of fabric equal to length of board plus 4½" (11.5 cm). Center board on wrong side of fabric.

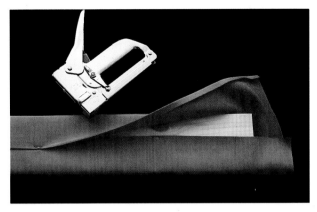

2) Staple one long edge of fabric to board, placing staples about 8" (20.5 cm) apart; do not staple within 6" (15 cm) of ends. Wrap fabric around board; fold under ⅜" (1 cm) on long edge, and staple to board, placing staples about 6" (15 cm) apart.

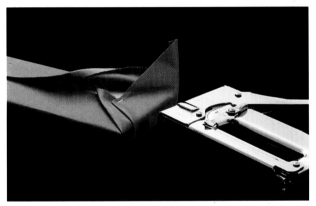

3) Miter fabric at corners on side of board with unfolded edge of fabric; finger-press. Staple miters in place near raw edge.

4) Miter fabric at corner on side of board with folded edge of fabric; finger-press. Fold excess fabric under at end of board; staple near fold.

How to Install a Mounting Board Using Angle Irons

1) Screw angle irons into covered mounting board, using #8 gauge ¾" (2 cm) pan-head screws. Hold board at desired placement, making sure that it is level; mark screw holes on wall or window frame, using pencil.

2) Remove angle irons from board. Secure angle irons to wall, using ⅛" (3 mm) L (long) molly bolts (page 26) or ¾" (2 cm) pan-head screws.

3) Mount window treatment onto mounting board, using staples. Place mounting board on installed angle irons. Screw angle irons into mounting board.

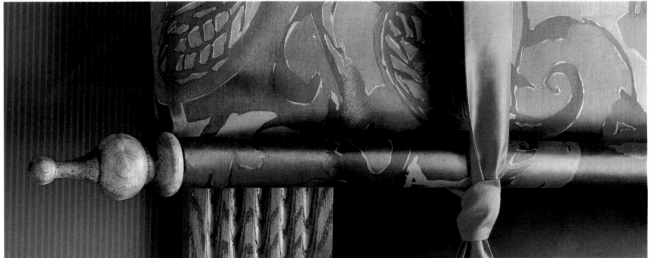

Outside mounted stagecoach valance has side returns; finials may be added at ends of wood pole, if desired.

Stagecoach Valances

This stationary, tailored top treatment features decorative ties and resembles the curtains used in the stagecoaches of the past. The valance may be lined with matching or contrasting fabric. The lining shows when the stagecoach valance is rolled at the lower edge.

A stagecoach valance is attached to a mounting board and is frequently mounted inside the window frame. When an inside mount is used, the finished width of the valance is ¼" (6 mm) less than the measurement inside the window frame, and the window treatment is attached to a 1" × 1" (2.5 × 2.5 cm) mounting board.

For an outside mount, side returns are added to the valance. The return is the distance from the wall to the front edge of the mounting board. The mounting board can either be mounted at the top of the window frame or on the wall above the window. The finished width of the valance should be at least 2" (5 cm) wider than the outside measurement of the window frame or 2" (5 cm) wider than the width of an undertreatment.

The ties are usually spaced 24" to 36" (61 to 91.5 cm) apart. If they are spaced farther apart, the valance fabric may buckle between the ties. If possible, plan the placement of the ties so they will be aligned with any existing vertical lines in the window.

✄ Cutting Directions

If this treatment is used on a window that is wider than the fabric width, railroad the fabric whenever possible (page 21). If the fabric cannot be railroaded, plan the placement of the seams so they will be concealed under the ties.

For an inside mount, the cut width of the face fabric is equal to the finished width of the valance plus 1" (2.5 cm) for seam allowances. For an outside mount, the cut width of the face fabric is equal to the finished width of the valance plus two times the return plus 1" (2.5 cm) for seam allowances.

The cut length of the face fabric is equal to the finished length plus the width of the mounting board plus 12" (30.5 cm) for a rolled effect at the lower edge plus 1" (2.5 cm) for seam allowances.

Cut the matching or contrasting lining the same size as the face fabric.

Cut two fabric strips for each tie location, with the cut width of each strip two times the finished width of the tie plus ½" (1.3 cm) for seam allowances. The finished width of the ties in the photos is 2" (5 cm). The fabric strips may be cut on the crosswise grain, with the cut length of the strips equal to the width of the fabric. Cut fabric to cover the mounting board (page 29).

YOU WILL NEED

Decorator fabric for valance and mounting board.

Matching or contrasting fabric for lining.

Contrasting fabric for ties.

1⅜" (3.5 cm) wood pole, cut to finished width of valance after it is stitched.

Mounting board, cut ¼" (6 mm) shorter than the finished width of valance after it is stitched. For inside mount, use 1" × 1" (2.5 × 2.5 cm) board. For outside mount, use a board at least 2" (5 cm) wider than projection of window frame or undertreatment.

Heavy-duty stapler; staples.

Angle irons, one for each end and one for every 45" (115 cm) interval across the width of the mounting board; pan-head screws or molly bolts (page 28) for outside mount.

Pan-head screws (page 28) for inside mount.

How to Sew an Inside-mounted Stagecoach Valance

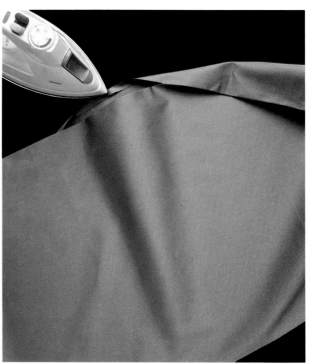

1) Seam fabric widths as necessary. Place face fabric and lining right sides together, matching raw edges. Stitch ½" (1.3 cm) seams around all sides; leave an 8" (20.5 cm) opening at center of upper edge for turning. Trim corners diagonally.

2) Turn valance right side out. Press edges, folding in seam allowances at center opening.

3) Cut two 3" (7.5 cm) circles. Attach to ends of wood pole, using fabric glue or spray adhesive.

4) Hold pole firmly against table; using pencil, draw line on pole where it touches table.

5) Center pole on right side of valance at lower edge; staple in place, aligning lower edge of valance to marked line on pole.

6) Roll up valance to desired finished length. Anchor pole in place with pins.

7) Fold fabric strips for ties in half lengthwise, right sides together. Stitch long edge and one short end, using ¼" (6 mm) seam allowance. Trim diagonally across corners, turn tie right side out, and press. Two ties are used at each placement.

8) Mark desired placement of ties at upper edge of valance. Staple valance to covered mounting board (page 29), aligning upper edge of valance to back edge of board. Do not place staples at markings for ties.

(Continued on next page)

How to Sew an Inside-mounted Stagecoach Valance (continued)

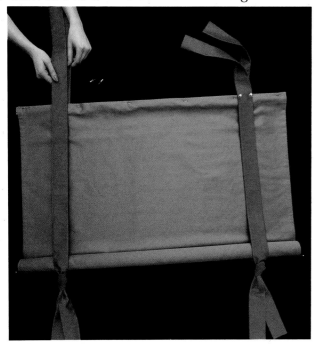

9) Sandwich valance between two ties at placement marks; tack in place, using map tacks Tie finished ends; adjust length of ties from upper edge, for desired effect, making sure all ties are the same length. Staple ties to board. Trim excess ties at top.

10) Mount valance by screwing board inside window frame, using #8 gauge 1½" (3.8 cm) pan-head screws. Predrill the holes, using ⅛" (3 mm) drill bit.

How to Sew an Outside-mounted Stagecoach Valance

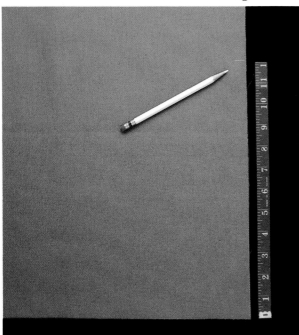

1) Seam fabric widths as necessary. Fold face fabric in half lengthwise, right sides together. At sides, mark a line 12½" (31.8 cm) from lower edge; this is the amount needed for rolled effect plus seam allowance.

2) Draw line in from side at marked line, the amount of one return. Draw line, parallel to side, down to lower edge; cut out section through both layers. The cut width at lower edge should now be the finished width of valance plus 1" (2.5 cm). Repeat for lining.

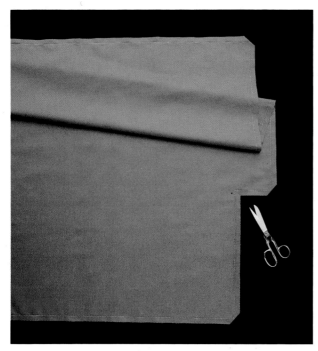

3) Place face fabric and lining right sides together, matching raw edges. Stitch ½" (1.3 cm) seams around all sides; leave an 8" (20.5 cm) opening at center of upper edge for turning. Clip and trim corners.

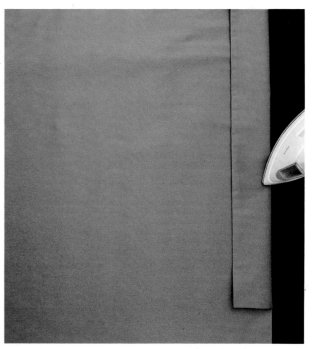

4) Turn valance right side out. Press edges, folding in seam allowances at center opening. Press returns lightly. Complete steps 3 to 7 on pages 32 and 33.

5) Mark desired placement of ties at upper edge of valance. Staple valance to covered mounting board (page 29), aligning upper edge of valance to back edge of board and centering upper edge on board, with returns extending at ends of board. Do not place staples at markings for ties.

6) Miter corners of returns; staple in place. Finish valance with ties, as in step 9, opposite. Mount as on pages 28 and 29.

Handkerchief Valances

This easy, tailored valance features a 3" (7.5 cm) band at the lower edge, which is simply an extension of the contrasting lining. The valance can be used alone or over another window treatment, such as blinds or underdraperies. It works well for small windows, without being overpowering, but this banded styling is also attractive on larger windows.

A handkerchief valance should be mounted as an outside mount (pages 28 and 29). The board can either be mounted at the top of the window frame or on the wall above the window. The finished width of the valance should be at least 2" (5 cm) wider than the outside measurement of the window frame or undertreatment; the finished width does not include the fabric drop at the sides of the valance.

✂ Cutting Directions

The cut width of the outer fabric is equal to the length of the mounting board plus two times the finished length of the valance plus 1" (2.5 cm) for seam allowances. The fabric may be railroaded if the design is not directional (page 21). Fabric that cannot be railroaded will require piecing if the cut width of the valance is wider than the fabric width; when the fabric is pieced, add the necessary extra width for seam allowances. To determine the cut length of the outer fabric, add the width of the mounting board to the desired finished length of the valance; then

subtract 2" (5 cm) from this measurement to allow for seam allowances and for a 3" (7.5 cm) contrasting band at the lower edge.

Cut the contrasting lining the same width as the outer fabric. To determine the cut length of the lining, add the width of the mounting board to the desired finished length of the valance; then add 4" (10 cm) to this measurement to allow for seam allowances and for a 3" (7.5 cm) contrasting band at the lower edge.

Cut fabric to cover the mounting board (page 29).

YOU WILL NEED

Decorator fabric in two contrasting colors for outer fabric and lining.

Mounting board, cut to the desired finished width of valance. Mounting board must be at least 2" (5 cm) wider than projection of window frame or undertreatment.

Angle irons, one for each end and one for every 45" (115 cm) interval across the width of the mounting board.

Heavy-duty stapler; staples.

Pan-head screws or molly bolts (page 28).

How to Sew a Handkerchief Valance

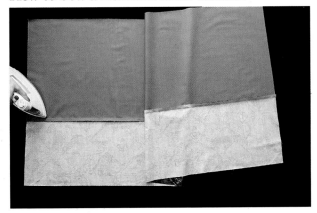

1) Seam fabric widths, if necessary. Place outer fabric and lining right sides together, matching the lower edges; stitch ½" (1.3 cm) seam. Press seam toward outer fabric.

2) Place outer fabric and lining right sides together, matching upper edges. Stitch ½" (1.3 cm) seams at sides and upper edge; leave an 8" (20.5 cm) opening at center of upper edge for turning. Trim corners diagonally. Press seam allowances open at edges.

3) Turn valance right side out. Press edges, folding in seam allowances at center opening.

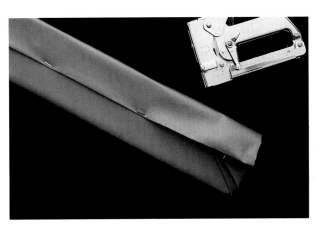

4) Cover mounting board with fabric (page 29); staple fabric in place at 4" (10 cm) intervals, folding under raw edges.

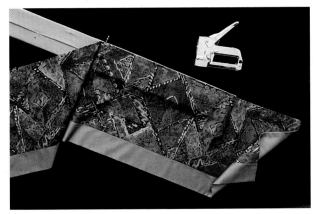

5) Mark center of mounting board; mark center of valance at upper edge. Place valance, right side up, on mounting board, aligning upper edge of valance to back edge of board; match center markings. Near back edge, staple valance to board at center. Working from center to sides, staple valance to board at 4" (10 cm) intervals, with one staple close to each end.

6) Screw angle irons to bottom of mounting board, positioning one at each end and spacing them at 45" (115 cm) intervals. Install valance on window frame or wall (pages 28 and 29). Adjust the drape at ends of valance.

Rod-sleeve Valances

Make quick and easy rod-sleeve valances by simply shirring fabric over a wide curtain rod. Tapered headings are added to the basic plain rod sleeve to create many different styles. This ruffled top treatment works well over shirred draperies for a feminine look, but may also be used with tailored blinds or pleated shades. The headings may be made from fabric that either matches or contrasts with the fabric for the rod sleeves.

For a dramatic top treatment, two or more drapery rods, covered with plain or tapered-heading rod sleeves, can be grouped together. When two rods are mounted next to each other, there is a small space between the rods, due to the mounting brackets. To fill in any space between the rods and prevent a light gap, a ½" (1.3 cm) ruffle is added to one of the rod sleeves and tucked behind the rods when the top treatment is mounted. For best results in preventing a light gap between the rods, add the ruffle to the lower edge of the upper rod sleeve.

✂ Cutting Directions

For either a plain rod sleeve or a rod sleeve with one heading, the cut length of the sleeve is equal to twice the width of the drapery rod plus 1" (2.5 cm) for ease and 1" (2.5 cm) for seam allowances. To add

The tapered heading at the top of this rod sleeve adds height above the window frame.

The heading can form a ruffle at the bottom of the rod sleeve by turning the top treatment upside down. A second drapery rod with a plain rod sleeve is used for a more pronounced effect.

a ½" (1.3 cm) ruffle between closely mounted rods, add an extra 1" (2.5 cm) to the cut length. The cut width of the rod sleeve is equal to three times the length of the drapery rod.

If you are making a rod sleeve with two headings, cut separate sections for the front and back of the sleeve, with the cut length of each equal to the width of the rod plus 1" (2.5 cm) for ease and 1" (2.5 cm) for seam allowances. If desired, the back of the rod sleeve may be cut from lining fabric. For each front and back, the cut width is equal to three times the length of the rod.

The cut length of a tapered heading is equal to twice the finished length of the heading plus 1" (2.5 cm) for seam allowances. The cut width of the heading is the same as the cut width of the rod sleeve. Tapered headings may be from matching or contrasting fabric.

YOU WILL NEED

Decorator fabric; one or two colors may be used.

Wide curtain rods, one for each rod sleeve.

Contemporary metal pole sets, if desired, for multiple-rod treatments.

Tapered headings are used at both the top and bottom of this rod sleeve for a different look.

Multiple drapery rods are used together to create a dramatic top treatment. In the treatment shown here, wide curtain rods are covered with rod sleeves and the contemporary metal pole sets are left uncovered.

How to Sew a Plain Rod Sleeve

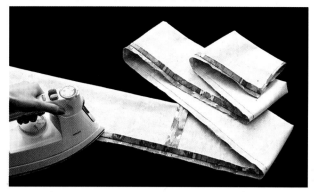

1) Seam fabric widths together. Press seams open. Stitch double ¼" (6 mm) side hems. Fold rod sleeve in half lengthwise, with right sides together and raw edges even. Stitch ½" (1.3 cm) seam; press open.

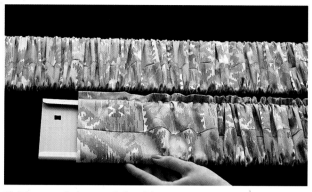

2) Turn rod sleeve right side out; press so seam is centered on back of sleeve. If ruffle is required to prevent a light gap on multiple-rod treatment (page 38), stitch ½" (1.3 cm) from folded edge. Insert drapery rod, gathering fabric evenly.

How to Sew a Rod Sleeve with One Heading

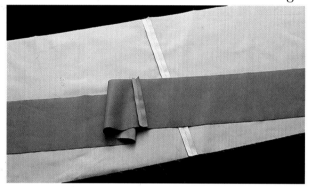

1) Seam fabric widths together for rod sleeve and heading. Press seams open.

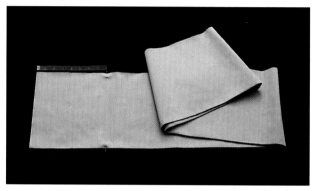

2) Fold heading in half lengthwise, *wrong* sides together; press foldline. Then fold in half crosswise; measure from ends a distance equal to twice the depth of return, and pin-mark. For example, for 4" (10 cm) return, pin-mark 8" (20.5 cm) from ends.

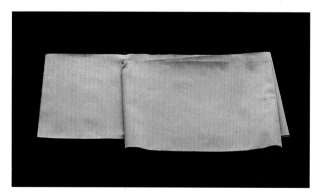

3) Determine one-third the distance from pin mark at return to crosswise foldline; measure this distance from crosswise foldline, and pin-mark. This is where tapering will begin.

4) Measure from lengthwise fold at return pin mark to desired height of heading plus ½" (1.3 cm) seam allowance; mark with pencil. For example, for 4" (10 cm) heading at return, mark 4½" (11.5 cm) from lengthwise fold.

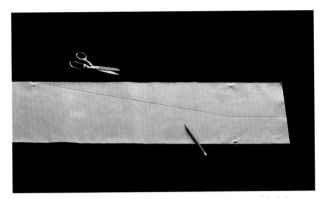

5) Draw straight line parallel to lengthwise fold, from ends of heading to pencil mark at return. Draw straight line at an angle from pencil mark at return to pin mark in center portion. Cut on marked lines.

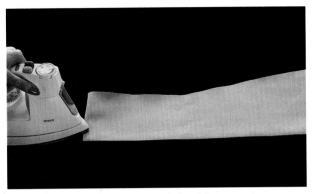

6) Fold heading lengthwise, right sides together; stitch ½" (1.3 cm) seams at ends. Turn heading right sides out; press.

7) Stitch double ¼" (6 mm) side hems on rod sleeve. Fold rod sleeve in half lengthwise, right sides together; sandwich heading in between, matching raw edges. Pin layers together, easing in seam allowances of heading, as necessary, so fabric lies flat. Stitch ½" (1.3 cm) seam.

8) Turn right side out; press. If a ruffle is required to prevent a light gap on multiple-rod treatment (page 38), stitch ½" (1.3 cm) from folded edge. Insert drapery rod, gathering fabric evenly.

How to Sew a Rod Sleeve with Two Headings

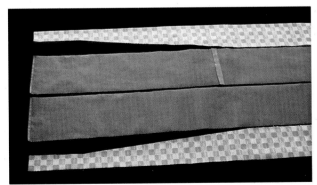

1) Seam fabric widths together for headings and front and back of rod sleeve. Press seams open. Make two headings as in steps 2 to 6, opposite. Stitch double ¼" (6 mm) side hems in front and back of rod sleeve.

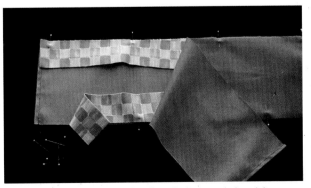

2) Place front and back of rod sleeve right sides together; sandwich headings in between, matching raw edges. Pin layers together, easing in seam allowances of headings, as necessary, so fabric lies flat. Stitch ½" (1.3 cm) seams. Turn right side out; press. Insert drapery rod, gathering fabric evenly.

Sunburst Curtains

A sunburst curtain dresses a Palladian window while diffusing the light. Designed to perfectly outline the arch shape, this sheer rod-pocket curtain is custom-fitted for your window.

Flexible plastic tubing, which shapes easily to curve around the window opening, is inserted into the rod pocket at the upper edge. Drapery cord, inserted into the opposite casing, holds the gathers at the center. A large rosette (pages 80 and 81) is used to finish the treatment.

Trace the shape of the inside window frame onto paper to make a pattern. Fitting adjustments can be made on the curtain, using the pattern, before it is installed.

✂ Cutting Directions

The cut width of the fabric is equal to one and one-half to two times the measurement of the curved line on the pattern, depending on the fullness desired. Railroad the fabric whenever possible to prevent seams (page 21).

To determine the cut length of the fabric, divide the length of the lower straight line on the pattern by two; then add 4½" (11.5 cm). This allows for a double ½" (1.3 cm) heading and a double 1" (2.5 cm) rod pocket at the outer edge, a double ½" (1.3 cm) casing at the center, and ½" (1.3 cm) for ease.

YOU WILL NEED

Sheer drapery fabric for curtain and rosette.

⅜" (1 cm) flexible plastic tubing (page 27), cut to fit curve at inside edge of window frame.

Sockets for ⅜" (1 cm) round rodding.

1" (2.5 cm) cup hooks; one for every 8" to 10" (20.5 to 25.5 cm) around curve of window, plus one for center of sunburst.

Nylon drapery cord; binder clips or clamps.

How to Sew and Install a Sunburst Curtain

1) Seam fabric widths, if necessary. Press under ½" (1.3 cm) twice at sides; stitch to make double-fold hems. Press under 1½" (3.8 cm) twice at upper edge; stitch rod pocket close to first fold, then 1" (2.5 cm) away. Press under and stitch double ½" (1.3 cm) rod pocket on lower edge.

2) Tie safety pin to one end of drapery cord; thread through casing at lower edge. Pull up cord as tightly as possible, and tie ends together; trim excess cord. This becomes center of sunburst.

3) Insert plastic tubing into casing at upper edge, gathering fabric. Pin or tape paper pattern to heavy cardboard or foam core board. Aligning heading of curtain to marked arc on pattern, clamp ends of tubing to cardboard; distribute gathers evenly and pin heading in place. Clamp center at lower edge.

4) Pull curtain taut toward center to remove slack, using double strand of thread. Cover center with a small half-circle of matching fabric, if necessary for neater appearance on outside of window treatment. Make rosette (pages 80 and 81); hand-stitch to center.

5) Screw sockets at ends of bottom window frame. Screw cup hooks into window frame at 8" to 10" (20.5 to 25.5 cm) intervals around arch, with hook openings facing into the room; position all cup hooks the same distance from edge of window frame. Screw one cup hook at center of bottom window frame.

6) Insert ends of tubing into sockets. Snap tubing into cup hooks around inside curve of window. Hook center of sunburst into cup hook at center of bottom window frame. It may be necessary to trim tubing to fit around window.

Scarf Swags

Scarf swags are an adaptation of the traditional swag window treatment, which consists of a swag draped across the top of the window, and cascades draped at the sides. A scarf swag can look like an elegant, traditional window treatment or can have a more contemporary, unstructured look. Scarf swags are suitable for nearly any size or shape of window, including arch windows.

The scarf swag is created from a long, lined rectangle of fabric, and is folded and draped at the window. The swag can be shaped to form rosettes at the corners of the treatment, using special U-shaped swag holders, or can be draped over tieback holders.

The swag holders or tieback holders may be installed at the outer corners of the window frame or on the wall, positioned up and out from the corners. For arch windows, shown opposite, the brackets can be installed symmetrically or asymmetrically around the arch of the window.

After deciding on the placement of the brackets, determine the length of the cascades at the sides of the window. For good proportion, cascades are often two-thirds the length of the window or end at the window sill. On large windows, they may be floor-length, or even longer, to "puddle" onto the floor. An asymmetrical look can be achieved by making one cascade noticeably longer than the other.

Mediumweight decorator fabric, such as chintz and sateen, is recommended. Avoid heavyweight fabrics, because they do not drape well and may not fit into a swag holder. Select a contrasting lining to accent the folds of the cascades. If a patterned fabric with a one-way design is used, the fabric for one cascade must be turned in the opposite direction and stitched to the swag portion of the treatment.

If the swag holders can be seen from the side view, cover the extensions of the brackets with rod panels for a more finished appearance. The cascade-length panels are placed over the extensions before the brackets are installed.

✂ Cutting Directions

Cut outer and lining fabrics the length calculated, below. The entire width of both fabrics is used; if outer fabric and lining are of two different widths, cut the wider fabric to match the narrower width.

If rod panels are desired for the brackets at the top of the cascades, cut two pieces of fabric for each rod panel, 7" (18 cm) wide by the length of cascade plus 1¾" (4.5 cm) for the rod pocket and the seam allowance. One piece may be cut from the outer fabric and one from the lining, or both pieces may be cut from the outer fabric.

YOU WILL NEED

Decorator fabric and contrasting lining.

Swag holders or tieback holders (page 27).

Drapery hooks, one per rosette; or wire.

How to Calculate Yardage for a Scarf Swag

Drape cord or tape measure across window, between swag holders or tieback holders, to simulate the planned shape of each swag. Add desired length of cascades to this measurement. For swag with rosettes, add 24" (61 cm) for each rosette.

How to Sew a Scarf Swag

1) Place outer fabric and lining right sides together. At one selvage, measure in 18" (46 cm) from each end of fabric; draw a line from these points diagonally to the corners of the opposite selvage. Trim away triangular pieces of fabric at each end.

2) Stitch around all four sides in ½" (1.3 cm) seam, leaving 12" (30.5 cm) opening at center for turning. Press seams open. Turn right side out; stitch opening closed. Press edges.

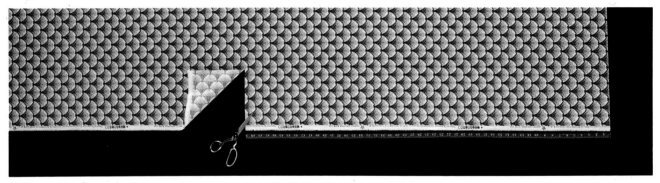

Fabric with one-way design. 1) Determine length of one cascade from lower edge up to tieback holder or swag holder; add 1" (2.5 cm) to this measurement. Measure this distance from one end of fabric; cut across width.

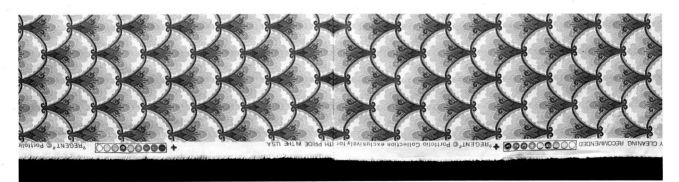

2) Turn fabric so design goes in opposite direction; stitch ½" (1.3 cm) seam. Seam will be concealed in rosette.

How to Sew a Rod Panel

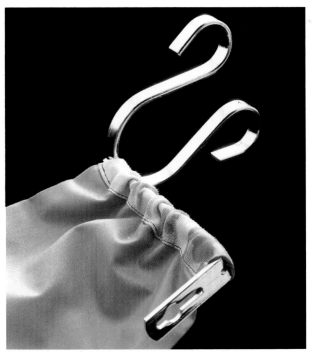

1) Place two rod panel pieces right sides together. Stitch around long sides and lower edge in ½" (1.3 cm) seam. Clip corners; turn right side out, and press. Fold under ¼" (6 mm) at upper edge to wrong side; then fold under 1" (2.5 cm). Stitch near second fold, forming rod pocket.

2) Slide rod pocket over extension of swag holder. Mount bracket onto wall or window frame.

How to Fold and Install a Scarf Swag

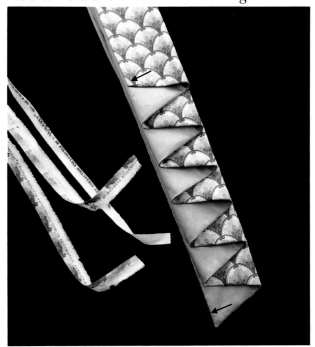

1) Lay scarf swag on long surface, such as floor, with lining side up. Accordion-fold entire width of swag in about 4" (10 cm) folds, beginning at longer side; both edges must face in same direction (arrows).

2) Tie folded swag with remnants of fabric every 18" to 24" (46 to 61 cm). This keeps folds in place, making swag easier to handle during installation.

(Continued on next page)

3) Place swag over bracket extensions, with shorter side facing down and in toward window. Drape folded swag portion the amount planned. If window treatment is to be symmetrical, check to see that cascade lengths are even. Remove ties.

4) Pull gently on lower folds for a deeper swag; pull gently on upper folds, toward brackets, to decrease amount of draping at top of swag. Adjust folds as desired; secure at brackets, using safety pins.

5) Measure down from bracket 24" (61 cm). Fold this 24" (61 cm) portion of fabric in half, forming 12" (30.5 cm) loop, with shorter side facing forward; do not twist swag. Bring fabric through U-portion of bracket, as shown; widen U-portion, if necessary for thickness of fabric. Keep fabric in accordion folds, with shorter side and contrasting folds facing window.

6) Adjust rosette portion so cascades are even in length if window treatment is to be symmetrical. Gently squeeze U-portion of bracket closed at the top as much as possible, to prevent rosette from sliding out of bracket during shaping. Secure top of bracket with a piece of wire or a drapery hook.

7) Pull the inside fold in middle of fabric loop, spreading fabric apart.

8) Form the rosette by continuing to pull out the fabric folds.

9) Tuck top and bottom of rosette back into bracket to round out the rosette, preventing peaks. Secure rosette as necessary with pins.

10) Adjust folds of cascades as necessary to achieve desired drape.

Covered Poles & Finials

Fabric-covered drapery poles and ball finials add a designer touch to scarf swags and other window treatments. Use unfinished wood poles and finials. The poles may be covered with either shirred or flat fabric.

A smooth covered rod is used to support the scarf swag shown at right. Twisted welting, draped with the swag, is also used to embellish the coordinating covered finial. A shirred covered rod is featured with rod-pocket curtains and covered finials with ruffles (inset, right).

✄ Cutting Directions

The cut length of the rod sleeve is equal to the rod circumference plus 1½" (3.8 cm) for 1⅜" (3.5 cm) diameter wood poles, or the circumference plus 1¾" (4.5 cm) for 2" (5 cm) wood poles.

For a flat rod sleeve, the cut width of the rod sleeve is equal to the length of the wood pole. For a shirred rod sleeve, the cut width is two or three times the length of the wood pole.

Cut the fabric circles for the finials as on page 52 or 53.

YOU WILL NEED

Decorator fabric.

Wood pole set with ball finials.

Brackets designed to be used with Cirmosa® rods.

Cord, braid, or ribbon trim for finials.

Fabric glue.

Tacks; or heavy-duty stapler and staples.

How to Make a Smooth Covered Pole

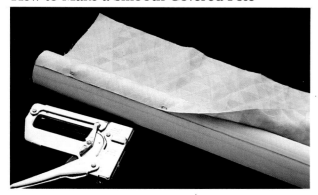

1) Mark line on wood pole, as in step 4, page 32. Staple or tack one edge of fabric to pole, aligning raw edge with marked line.

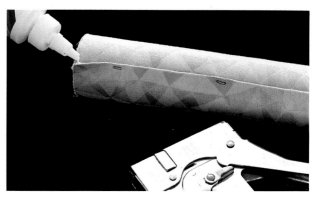

2) Wrap fabric snugly around pole. Fold under raw edge; staple or tack in place. Apply glue around end of pole so rod sleeve will adhere. Allow glue to dry.

How to Make a Shirred Covered Pole

Sew plain rod sleeve as on page 40, except do not stitch side hems. Insert drapery rod, gathering fabric evenly. Apply glue around end of wood pole, so rod sleeve will adhere. Allow glue to dry.

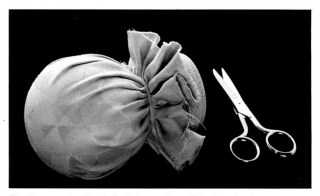

Alternate method for rod-pocket curtain. Sew plain rod sleeve for exposed portion of wood pole only, as on page 40, except do not stitch side hems. Insert drapery rod, gathering fabric evenly. Apply glue to pole at ends of rod sleeve; allow to dry. Curtain covers remainder of pole.

How to Make a Covered Finial

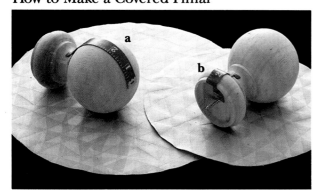

1) Measure ball portion of finial from top of finial to neck **(a);** cut one fabric circle for each finial, with a radius 1" (2.5 cm) longer than measurement. Measure the crown portion of finial from neck to base **(b);** cut one fabric circle for each finial, with radius 1" (2.5 cm) longer than measurement.

2) Center ball of finial on first fabric circle; wrap fabric around ball to neck of finial. Secure fabric at neck with rubber band, adjusting fullness evenly; trim to within ½" (1.3 cm) of rubber band.

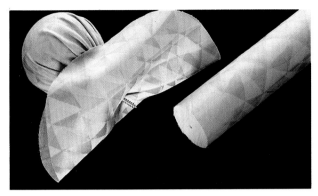

3) Pierce center of second fabric circle; twist fabric over screw. Attach finial to wood pole.

4) Apply bead of glue around neck. Wrap second circle to neck, securing with second rubber band and adjusting gathers evenly; allow glue to dry. Trim fabric close to rubber band. Cover rubber band with cord, braid, or ribbon trim.

How to Make a Covered Finial with a Ruffle

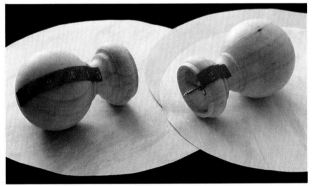

1) Measure ball of finial and cut one fabric circle for each finial, as in step 1 for covered finial, opposite. Measure crown of finial as in step 1; cut two fabric circles for each finial, with radius of each circle equal to measurement plus depth of ruffle plus ½" (1.3 cm).

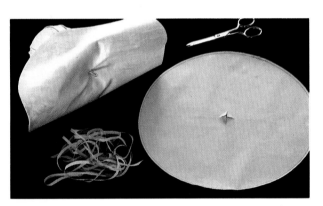

2) Place fabric circles for crown right sides together. Stitch in ¼" (6 mm) seam; trim to ⅛" (3 mm). Slash 1" (2.5 cm) "X" through one layer of fabric at center. Turn right side out through slash; press. Finish as in steps 2 to 4 for covered finial, opposite, but do not trim ruffle.

How to Install a Covered Pole with Finials

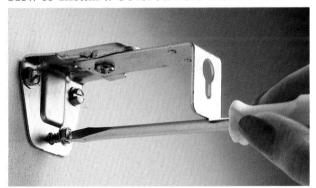

1) Attach brackets to the wall or window frame, using molly bolts (page 26) or pan-head screws (page 28).

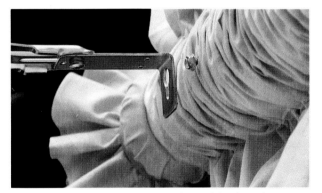

2) Attach screws to covered rod, positioning them same distance apart as keyhole openings on brackets. Hang covered rod on brackets.

Butterfly Swags

Butterfly swags have a soft, informal look. The edge of the valance is trimmed with a matching ruffle, and for easy construction, the swag is gathered with two-cord shirring tape.

Butterfly swags are attached to a mounting board. Determine the finished width of an inside-mounted or outside-mounted valance as for a stagecoach valance (page 31). When an outside mount is used, the sides of the mounting board will show, because the valance does not wrap around the sides. To make the board less noticeable, cover it with fabric that matches the valance. For good proportion, the center swagged portion is usually two-thirds or three-fourths the finished width.

✄ Cutting Directions

If this treatment is used on a window that is wider than the fabric width, railroad the fabric whenever possible, to avoid seaming. If the fabric cannot be railroaded, place the seams so they will be aligned with the shirring tape and concealed in the gathers.

Cut the decorator fabric and the lining the same size. The cut width of the fabrics is equal to the finished width of the valance plus 1" (2.5 cm) for the seam allowances minus twice the finished width of the ruffle. When the fabric is railroaded, the full width of the fabric is used for the cut length. Otherwise, the cut length of the fabric is 45" to 54" (115 to 137 cm),

giving a 15" to 18" (38 to 46 cm) drop length at the center of the swag.

For a 2½" (6.5 cm) self-lined ruffle, cut fabric strips 6" (15 cm) wide. To calculate the total cut length of the strips, multiply the distance around the sides and lower edge of the valance by two for double fullness, or by three for triple fullness. Piece the fabric strips together, as necessary.

Cut two pieces of shirring tape, with the length of each piece equal to the cut length of the valance minus the width of the mounting board.

YOU WILL NEED

Decorator fabric for valance and ruffle.

Lining fabric.

Two-cord shirring tape.

Mounting board, cut as for stagecoach valance (page 31).

Heavy-duty stapler; staples.

Angle irons; pan-head screws or molly bolts (page 28) for outside mount.

Pan-head screws (page 28) for inside mount.

How to Sew a Butterfly Swag

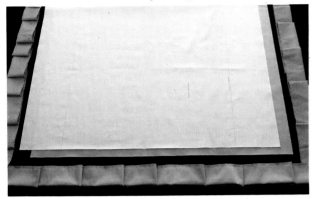

1) **Seam** the fabric widths together if fabric is not railroaded. Mark vertical placement lines for shirring tape on right side of lining. Fold pieced ruffle strip in half lengthwise, *wrong* sides together; press. Stitch gathering stitches by zigzagging over a cord, as on page 101, step 9.

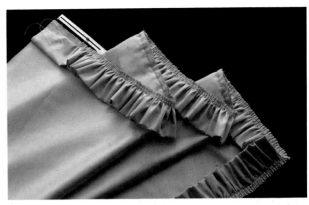

2) **Measure** distance around sides and lower edge of valance; divide into fourths, and pin-mark. Divide ruffle strip into fourths, and pin-mark. Pin ruffle to right side of valance, matching pin marks. Pull up gathering threads to fit; leave ruffle strip flat at upper edge for a distance equal to width of mounting board. Stitch a scant ½" (1.3 cm) from raw edges.

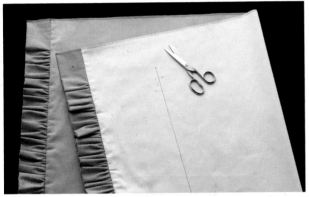

3) **Place** the lining and valance fabrics right sides together, matching raw edges; pin. Stitch around sides and lower edge of valance in ½" (1.3 cm) seam. Trim corners diagonally. Turn valance right side out; press. Finish upper edge.

4) **Fold** under ¼" (6 mm) on both ends of shirring tape pieces. Pin tape in place, starting at lower edge and centering it over marked lines on lining; tape will not reach upper edge. Stitch three rows of stitching on tape through all layers of fabric; stitch center row of stitching first, then along outer edges.

5) **Knot** cords at upper end of tape. Pull cords from lower end, gathering fabric to desired length. Check to see that both shirred tapes are the same length; knot ends, and conceal cords behind valance.

6) **Cover** the mounting board with matching fabric (page 29). Staple valance to board. Mount valance (pages 28 and 29.)

Rod-pocket Swags & Cascades

This swagged window treatment is not only easy to sew, but is also easier to install than most swags. Just insert the drapery rod into the rod pockets and adjust the gathers evenly. When a print fabric is used, choose one of the colors in the print as the accent color in the swags.

Swags may be used with or without cascades. Cascades add a more vertical appearance to the window treatment. When swags and cascades are used with underdraperies, make the cascades to match the draperies so they blend in, or make them from an accent color in the swags to contrast with the draperies.

Triple fullness is recommended for this window treatment. At this fullness, each cascade covers about 15" (38 cm) of the window width; each swag covers about 10" to 12" (25.5 to 30.5 cm) of the width. If you are not making cascades for the sides of the window, determine the number of swags you need by dividing the width of the window by 10" (25.5 cm); round up or down, if necessary, to the closest number. If you are making cascades, first subtract 30" (76 cm) from the width of the window; then divide the remaining width by 10" (25.5 cm) to determine the number of swags.

✄ Cutting Directions

To determine the depth of the rod pocket, add 1" (2.5 cm) ease to the width of the drapery rod. The cut length of each swag panel is equal to two times the desired finished length, two times the depth of the rod pocket, two times the depth of the heading, 3" (7.5 cm) for pouffing, and 1" (2.5 cm) for seam allowances.

One fabric width will make three swags. If two fabrics of different widths are being used, cut the wider fabric to the same width as the narrower one. Cut each fabric to the calculated length, and then cut lengthwise into thirds.

The short point of the cascades is equal to the finished length of the swags. The long point should be at least 12" (30.5 cm) longer than the short point, but may be two-thirds the length of the window, sill-length, or apron-length. If used with underdraperies, the long point is usually two-thirds the length of the draperies.

The cut length of the cascades is equal to the finished length at the long point, the depth of the rod pocket, the depth of the heading, and 2" (5 cm) for seam allowances. For each cascade, you will need one cut length of each of the two fabrics.

YOU WILL NEED

Decorator fabrics in two contrasting colors.

Flat drapery rod; projection of rod must be at least 2" (5 cm) more than projection of underdraperies or other undertreatment.

How to Sew Rod-pocket Swags

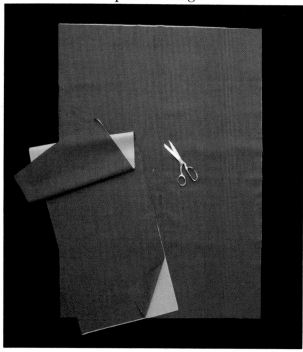

1) Place face fabric and lining right sides together. Mark width of fabric into three equal panels; cut.

2) Stitch panels of face fabric and lining together around all four sides in ½" (1.3 cm) seam, leaving 6" (15 cm) opening at upper edge for turning; trim corners. Turn right sides out; press.

3) Measure combined depth of rod pocket and heading from upper edge of panel; fold and press to lining side at this depth. Measure combined depth of rod pocket and heading from lower edge of panel; fold and press to face-fabric side at this depth.

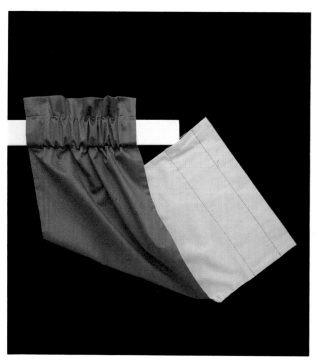

4) Stitch rod pockets. Insert drapery rod into rod pocket at upper edge. Then fold panel under, and insert drapery rod into rod pocket at lower edge. Repeat for remaining swag panels.

How to Sew Rod-pocket Cascades

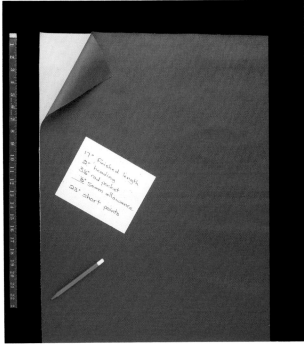

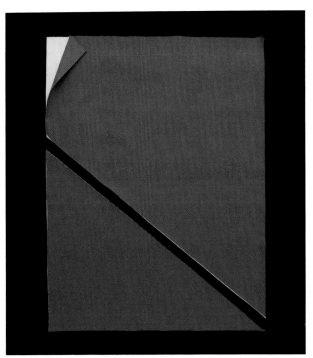

1) Place face fabric and lining right sides together. Determine length at short points by adding finished length of swag, depth of heading, depth of rod pocket, and ½" (1.3 cm) seam allowance. On inner sides of cascades, measure this distance from upper edge; mark short points.

2) Draw a line on each cascade from marking for short point to lower edge of outer side, or long point. Cut on marked line.

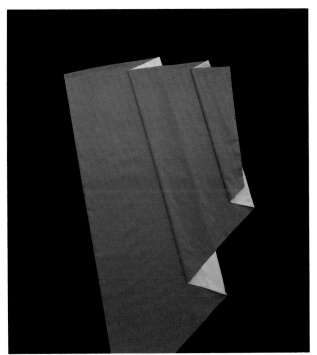

3) Stitch panels around all four sides in ½" (1.3 cm) seam, leaving 6" (15 cm) opening at upper edge for turning; trim corners. Turn right sides out; press.

4) Measure combined depth of rod pocket and heading from upper edges of cascades; fold and press to lining side at this depth. Stitch rod pockets. Insert drapery rod into rod pockets.

Pillows

Pillows

Pillows can add softness and texture to a room for a decorative finishing touch. Instructions for several pillow designs, from pillows with rosettes to pillows with knotted jumbo welting, are included on the following pages.

For most pillows, cut the pillow top and back 1" (2.5 cm) wider and longer than the finished size of the pillow. If using a pillow form, cut the fabric 1" (2.5 cm) wider and longer than the form. To prevent dog-eared corners on square or rectangular pillows, taper the corners of the fabric, opposite.

A zipper closure can be added to make it easier to clean the pillow cover. An invisible zipper can be inserted along one side for an inconspicuous closure; use the special zipper foot designed for applying invisible zippers.

If the pillow has welting, it may be easier to add a seam and insert the zipper on the pillow back. To make a zippered pillow cover that has a back seam, cut the pillow front 1" (2.5 cm) wider and longer than the finished size of the pillow, or 1" (2.5 cm) wider and longer than the pillow form. Cut one pillow back piece the width of the pillow front and 3¾" (9.5 cm) long; cut another piece, the width of the pillow front and 2¼" (6 cm) shorter than the length of the pillow front.

When the pillow cover is completed, insert a pillow form, or fill the cover with polyester fiberfill or quilt batting. Push fiberfill or batting into the corners and along the sides as necessary to fill out the pillow. Even when a pillow form is used, you may want to add fiberfill or batting to the corners and sides.

How to Prevent Dog-eared Corners

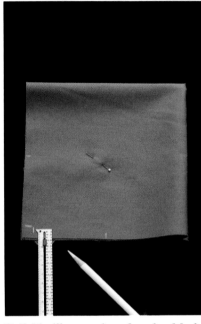

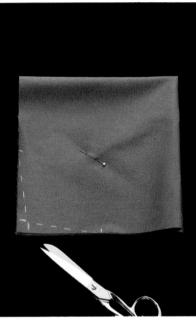

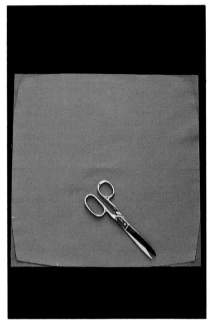

1) Fold pillow top into fourths. Mark a point halfway between corner and fold on each open side. At corner, mark a point ½" (1.3 cm) from each raw edge.

2) Mark lines, tapering from raw edges at center marks to mark at corner. Cut on marked lines.

3) Use pillow top as pattern for cutting pillow back so all corners are tapered. For zippered pillow cover, below, corners may be tapered on pillow back after the zipper is inserted.

How to Sew a Pillow with a Back Zipper

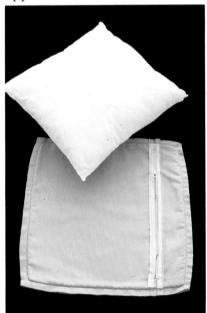

1) Cut pillow pieces, opposite. Stitch pillow back pieces together in ¾" (2 cm) seam, basting in zipper area. Apply zipper that is about 2" (5 cm) shorter than the finished width of the pillow. To prevent dog-eared corners, taper corners of pillow front and back, above.

2) Apply welting (pages 64 to 67) to pillow front, if desired. Pin pillow front to pillow back, right sides together; stitch ½" (1.3 cm) seam. Turn right side out.

3) Stuff pillow cover by inserting pillow form. Push polyester fiberfill or quilt batting into corners of the pillow and along sides as necessary to fill out pillow.

Welting

Many decorator pillows have welting to emphasize the edges. You can make welting by covering cording with fabric strips (opposite), or make gathered welting (pages 66 and 67). Or use purchased twisted welting (pages 68 and 69).

To make welting, cut fabric strips on the bias for greater flexibility around curved edges and corners. The bias strips do not have to be cut on the true bias. Strips that are cut at an angle less than 45 degrees provide the necessary flexibility but require less yardage. For economical use of fabric, the strips may be cut on the crosswise grain instead of the bias, but the welting may not be as smooth and may appear wrinkled.

The width of the fabric strips depends on the size of the cording. To determine how wide to cut the strips, wrap a piece of fabric around the cording. Pin it together, encasing the cording. Measure this distance and add 1" (2.5 cm) for seam allowances. Cut fabric strips to this width.

Cording, which comes on large spools, may have a tendency to curl or twist even after it is uncoiled from the spool. When sewing the welting, take care to smooth out the cording, removing any twists, to prevent the finished welting from appearing twisted.

How to Make and Attach Welting

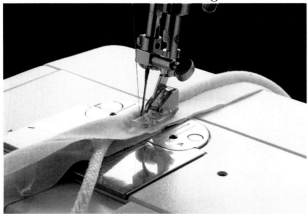

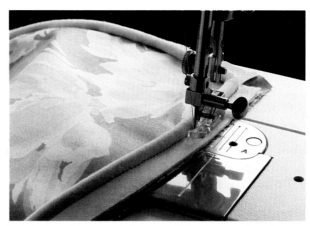

1) Cut fabric strips, opposite; seam strips together as necessary for desired length. Fold fabric strip around cording, wrong sides together, matching raw edges. Using a zipper foot, machine-baste close to cording; smooth cording as you sew, removing twists.

2) Stitch welting to right side of fabric over previous stitches, matching raw edges and starting 2" (5 cm) from end of welting; clip and ease welting at corners, or ease welting at curves.

3) Stop stitching 2" (5 cm) from point where ends of welting will meet. Cut off one end of welting so it overlaps the other end by 1" (2.5 cm).

4) Remove stitching from one end of welting, and trim ends of cording so they just meet.

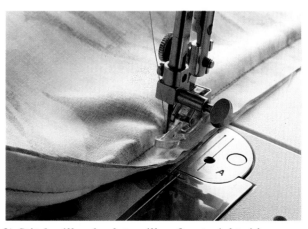

5) Fold under ½" (1.3 cm) of fabric on overlapping end of welting. Lap it around the other end; finish stitching welting to pillow front.

6) Stitch pillow back to pillow front, right sides together, using zipper foot; stitch inside previous stitching line, crowding stitches against welting. Leave opening on one side for turning, if pillow cover is not zippered.

Gathered Welting

Gathered welting is used for a shirred border on a pillow and adds textural interest. For a dramatic, bold effect, jumbo cording is used.

Cut a length of jumbo cording about 10" (25.5 cm) longer than the distance to be welted. Cut fabric strips for the gathered welting on the straight of grain. The width of the fabric strips depends on the size of the jumbo cording. To determine how wide to cut the strips, wrap a piece of fabric around the cording, and pin it together, encasing the cording. Measure this distance, and add 2" (5 cm) to allow for ease and seam allowances; cut straight-grain fabric strips to this width. The combined length of the strips should be two or three times the length of the cording to allow for the fullness of the gathers.

How to Make and Apply Gathered Welting

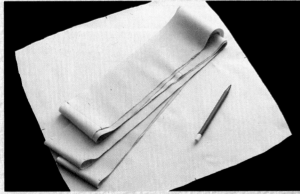

1) Stitch fabric strips together into a continuous circle. Divide fabric strip and outer edge of pillow into fourths; mark with water-soluble marking pen.

2) Fold strip around cording, wrong sides together, matching raw edges; secure cording to strip 4" (10 cm) from end, using safety pin. Using zipper foot, stitch about 10" to 12" (25.5 to 30.5 cm), stitching ⅜" (1 cm) from edge. Stop stitching, leaving needle in fabric.

3) Pull cording gently and push fabric strip back to end of cording until fabric behind needle is tightly gathered. Stitch 10" to 12" (25.5 to 30.5 cm) at a time, leaving 6" (15 cm) opening if welting has double fullness, or 9" (23 cm) opening if welting has triple fullness.

4) Pin gathered welting to right side of pillow front, matching raw edges and pin marks; distribute gathers evenly. Stitch ½" (1.3 cm) from raw edge, using zipper foot, leaving 3" (7.5 cm) unstitched at opening in gathered welting; ease welting at curves and corners. A tool, such as a seam ripper, is helpful for guiding the gathers.

5) Turn welting into finished position. Adjust cording at corners for a smooth fit around pillow. Mark a line on each end of cording so marked lines just meet. At marked lines, wrap ends of cording with transparent tape. Cut off excess cording on marked lines.

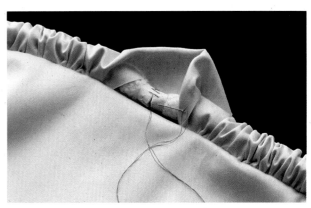

6) Hand-stitch ends of cording together, stitching through tape.

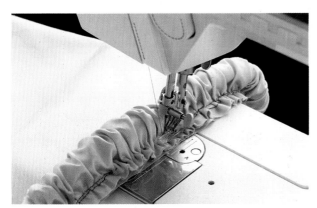

7) Fold fabric around cording at opening; stitch gathering threads at opening, and pull threads to gather remaining welting. Distribute gathers evenly. Stitch welting to fabric.

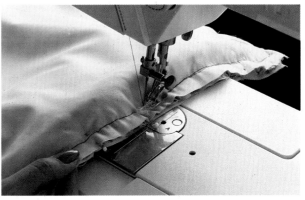

8) Stitch pillow back to pillow front, right sides together, using zipper foot; stitch inside previous stitching line. Leave opening on one side for turning, if pillow cover is not zippered.

Twisted Welting

Twisted welting, a decorative alternative to fabric-covered welting, has an attached tape, or lip, that can be stitched into the seams. Rayon welting, which has a shiny appearance, is more difficult to handle than cotton welting.

From the right side of the welting, the inner edge of the tape is not visible. For easier stitching and a more finished appearance on the front of the pillow, the welting is applied to the pillow back, right sides up. The ends of the welting can be twisted together to join them inconspicuously.

How to Attach Twisted Welting to a Pillow

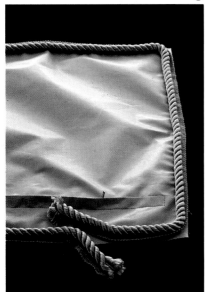

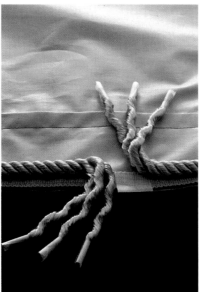

1) Stitch twisted welting to pillow back, using zipper foot, with right sides up and edge of welting tape aligned to raw edge of fabric. Leave 1½" (3.8 cm) unstitched between ends; leave 3" (7.5 cm) tails.

2) Remove stitching from welting tape on tails. Separate cords; wrap transparent tape around ends to prevent raveling. Trim welting tape to 1" (2.5 cm) from stitching; overlap ends and secure with transparent tape. Arrange cords so those at right turn up and those at left turn down.

3) Insert cords at right end under welting tape, twisting and pulling them down until welting is returned to its original shape. Secure in place, using transparent tape or pins.

4) Twist and pull cords at left end over cords at right end until the twisted ends look like continuous twisted welting; check both sides of welting.

5) Position zipper foot on left side of needle; this will allow you to stitch in the direction of the twists. Machine-baste through all layers to secure welting at seamline, or cords may be hand-basted in place, if desired.

6) Place pillow back on pillow front, right sides together. Stitch as close to welting as possible, using zipper foot. If pillow cover is not zippered, leave an opening on one side for turning. With pillow front facing up, stitch again, crowding stitches closer to welting.

Butterfly Pillows

This plump pillow trimmed with twisted welting has a dimensional effect. The butterfly pillow consists of two pillows, one square and one rectangular, tied together tightly at the center. The twisted welting is applied to the pillow back, for easier stitching and a more finished appearance on the front of the pillow. Fabric-covered welting can be substituted for the twisted welting, if desired. When fabric-covered welting is used, it is applied to the pillow front (pages 64 and 65).

✂ Cutting Directions

Cut two 15" × 19" (38 × 48.5 cm) rectangles, two 15" (38 cm) squares, and two 2" (5 cm) squares of decorator fabric.

YOU WILL NEED

1 yd. (0.95 m) decorator fabric.

4¼ yd. (3.9 m) twisted welting; or two colors of twisted welting, 2⅛ yd. (1.95 m) each.

One rectangular pillow form, 14" × 18" (35.5 × 46 cm).

One square pillow form, 14" (35.5 cm).

How to Sew a Butterfly Pillow

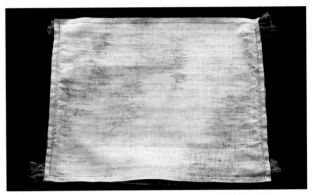

1) Pin 15" (38 cm) lengths of twisted welting to fabric, right sides up, along 15" (38 cm) sides of rectangular pillow back and two opposite sides of square pillow back. Remove the stitching from welting tape for 1" (2.5 cm) at ends. Untwist each end slightly, and curve cording into seam allowance; pin. Machine-baste welting in place, using zipper foot.

2) Pin rectangles, right sides together. With pillow back facing up, stitch around pillow, stitching as close as possible to welting on sides and stitching ½" (1.3 cm) seam on upper and lower edges; leave 8" (20.5 cm) opening at center of lower edge for turning.

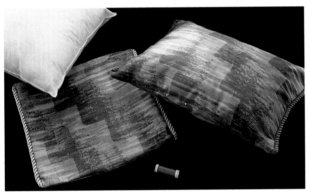

3) Repeat step 2 for square pillow. Insert pillow forms; slipstitch openings closed.

4) Remove welting tape from remaining welting. With square pillow centered over rectangular pillow, wrap welting tape around pillows twice, cinching them tightly; tie at bottom of pillows. Tuck ends of welting tape between pillows.

5) Cut remaining welting in half if using one color. Machine-stitch cords together at one end to right side of 2" (5 cm) fabric square, stitching ¼" (6 mm) from raw edge of fabric. Trim ends of welting. Fold square down and fold in all edges, enclosing ends of welting; hand-stitch. Twist welting tightly. Apply fabric square to other end.

6) Wrap welting around pillows twice. Tuck ends between pillows or under twisted welting.

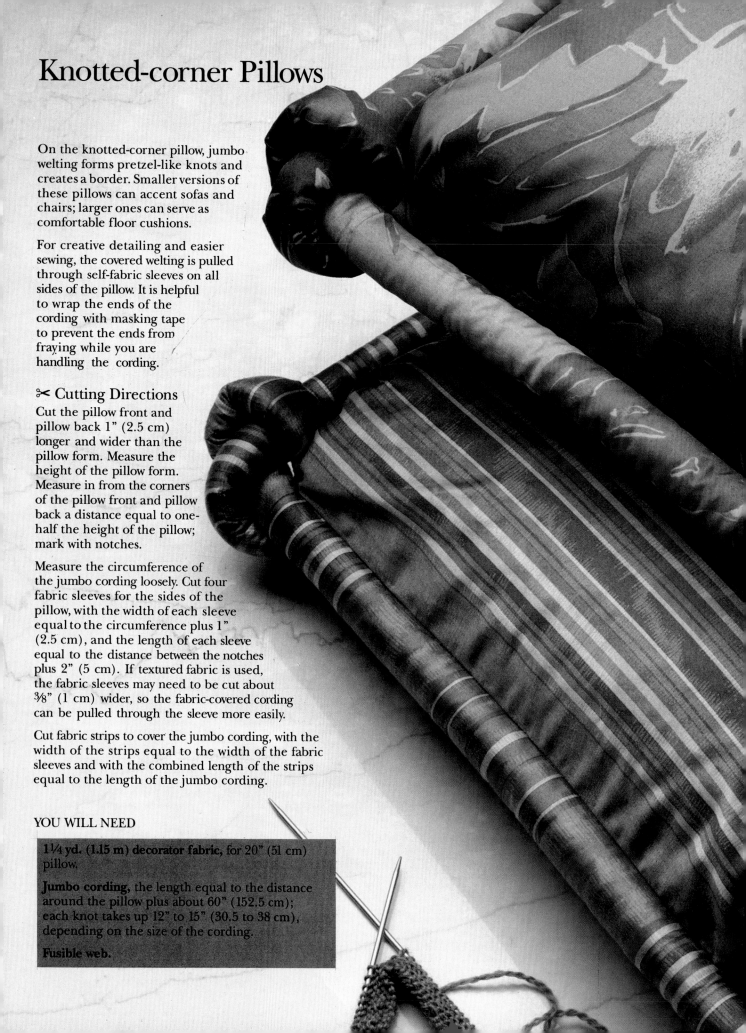

Knotted-corner Pillows

On the knotted-corner pillow, jumbo welting forms pretzel-like knots and creates a border. Smaller versions of these pillows can accent sofas and chairs; larger ones can serve as comfortable floor cushions.

For creative detailing and easier sewing, the covered welting is pulled through self-fabric sleeves on all sides of the pillow. It is helpful to wrap the ends of the cording with masking tape to prevent the ends from fraying while you are handling the cording.

✂ Cutting Directions

Cut the pillow front and pillow back 1" (2.5 cm) longer and wider than the pillow form. Measure the height of the pillow form. Measure in from the corners of the pillow front and pillow back a distance equal to one-half the height of the pillow; mark with notches.

Measure the circumference of the jumbo cording loosely. Cut four fabric sleeves for the sides of the pillow, with the width of each sleeve equal to the circumference plus 1" (2.5 cm), and the length of each sleeve equal to the distance between the notches plus 2" (5 cm). If textured fabric is used, the fabric sleeves may need to be cut about 3/8" (1 cm) wider, so the fabric-covered cording can be pulled through the sleeve more easily.

Cut fabric strips to cover the jumbo cording, with the width of the strips equal to the width of the fabric sleeves and with the combined length of the strips equal to the length of the jumbo cording.

YOU WILL NEED

1¼ yd. (1.15 m) decorator fabric, for 20" (51 cm) pillow.

Jumbo cording, the length equal to the distance around the pillow plus about 60" (152.5 cm); each knot takes up 12" to 15" (30.5 to 38 cm), depending on the size of the cording.

Fusible web.

How to Sew a Knotted-corner Pillow

1) Mark notches on pillow front and pillow back, as on page 72. Press under 1" (2.5 cm) on short ends of fabric sleeves; fuse in place, using fusible web.

2) Fold fabric sleeves in half lengthwise, wrong sides together; pin to pillow front between the notches, matching raw edges. Baste strips in place on seamline.

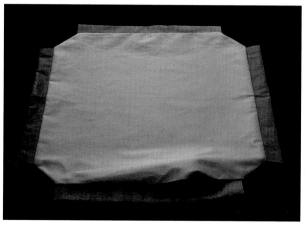

3) Pin pillow front to pillow back, right sides together. Stitch ½" (1.3 cm) seam on sides of pillow, stitching diagonally across corners between notches; leave an opening on one side for turning. Trim excess fabric at corners. Turn pillow cover right side out.

4) Fold fabric strip in half lengthwise, right sides together; stitch ½" (1.3 cm) seam. Turn right side out, using large safety pin or bodkin.

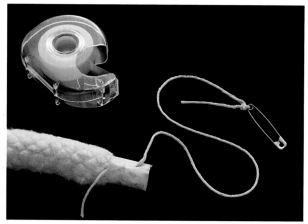

5) Cut piece of string the length of one side of pillow. Tie string around end of cording. Secure string to cording by wrapping it with tape. Attach safety pin or bodkin to end of string.

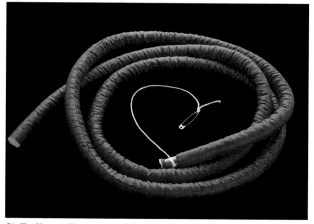

6) Pull cording through fabric strip to make welting. Tie string around end of welting; secure string to welting by wrapping it with tape.

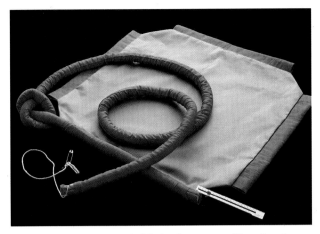

7) Pull welting through fabric sleeve on pillow, leaving 1" (2.5 cm) tail at beginning. Tie overhand knot at end of sleeve.

8) Pull welting through next sleeve; tie another overhand knot. Repeat with remaining sleeves.

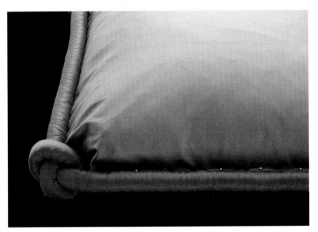

9) Insert pillow form, as on page 63, step 3; pin opening closed. Adjust all knots to same size. Turn seam on welting inward at knots.

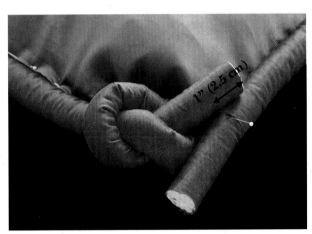

10) Cut off excess welting at end, so welting overlaps first sleeve 1" (2.5 cm), arrow. Mark welting at beginning of first sleeve.

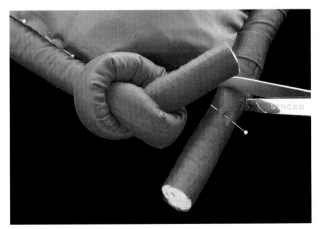

11) Pull end of welting out of first sleeve. Cut welting 1" (2.5 cm) beyond mark.

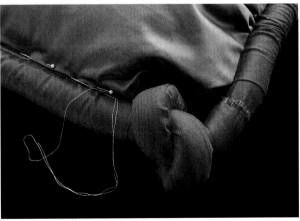

12) Whipstitch ends of welting together. Slide ends back into sleeve. Slipstitch opening on pillow closed.

Sunburst Pillows

Framed with a ruffle and welting, this half-circle pillow can be made in any size and is an interesting accent on sofas and beds. The pillow shown is made from a pattern 18" (46 cm) across and 11½" (29.3 cm) high and has a 3" (7.5 cm) finished ruffle. When twisted welting is used, it is applied to the pillow back over the ruffle, for easier stitching and a more finished appearance on the front of the pillow. When fabric-covered welting is used, it is applied to the pillow front.

✂ Cutting Directions

Cut the pillow front and pillow back, using the pattern, opposite. For the ruffle, cut fabric strips two times the finished width of the ruffle plus 1" (2.5 cm) for seam allowances. For triple fullness, the combined length of the fabric strips is equal to three times the measurement along the curved edge of the pattern.

YOU WILL NEED

¾ yd. (0.7 m) decorator fabric, for pillow shown.

1½ yd. (1.4 m) twisted welting with welting tape or lip; or fabric-covered welting (pages 64 and 65).

Polyester fiberfill.

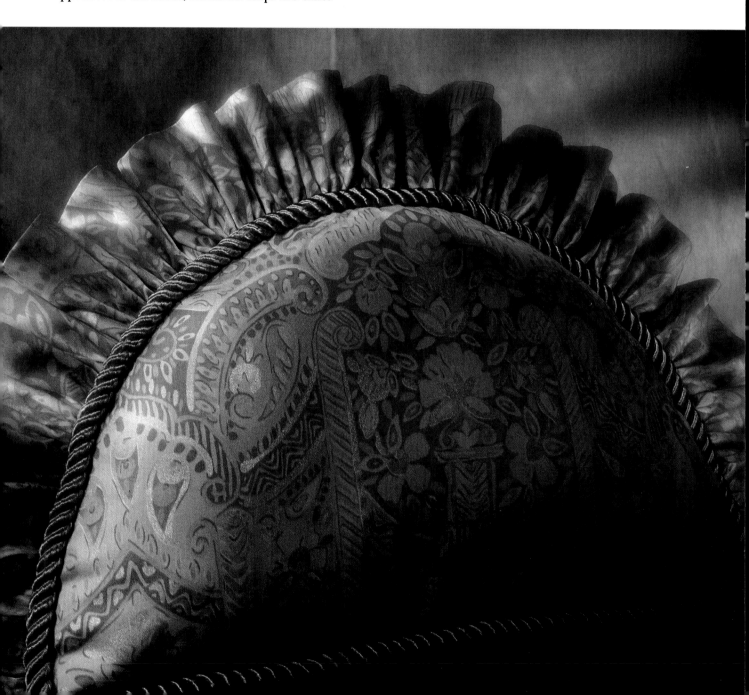

How to Make the Pattern for a Sunburst Pillow

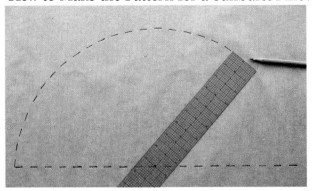

1) Draw a dotted line on paper equal to the desired diameter of circle. Using straightedge and pencil, mark half circle, measuring a distance equal to the radius from midpoint of dotted line.

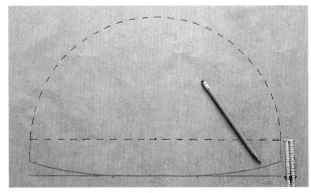

2) Extend lines straight down at sides for 1½" (3.8 cm). Draw line 2½"(6.5 cm) away from dotted line; divide into thirds, and mark. Draw slightly curved line between side and one-third markings. Cut on marked lines to complete pattern piece.

How to Sew a Sunburst Pillow

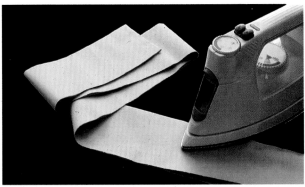

1) Stitch fabric strips together for ruffle in ¼" (6 mm) seams, right sides together. Fold pieced strip in half lengthwise, right sides together; stitch across ends in ¼" (6 mm) seam. Turn right side out; press. Stitch two rows of gathering threads on strip, ½" (1.3 cm) and ¼" (6 mm) from raw edge; or zigzag over cord as on page 101, step 9.

2) Divide strip and curved edges of pillow front and back into fourths; pin-mark. Place strip on curved edge of pillow back, right sides together, matching raw edges and pin marks; pull gathering threads to fit. Machine-baste ruffle, leaving pin marks in place.

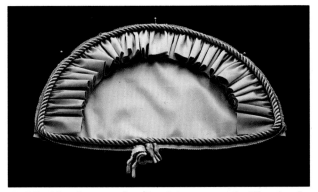

3) Machine-baste twisted welting around pillow back, over ruffle, and join ends as on pages 68 and 69. Or machine-baste fabric-covered welting around pillow front and join ends as on page 65.

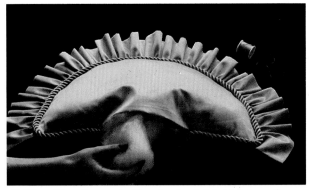

4) Pin pillow front to pillow back, right sides together, matching the pin marks. Stitch, using a zipper foot, crowding stitches against welting; leave 8" (20.5 cm) opening at bottom for turning. Stuff pillow with fiberfill, pushing it firmly into corners of pillow and along sides. Slipstitch opening closed.

Reversible Rosette Pillows

Perfect for the bedroom, a rosette pillow is simply a circular pillow cover tied around a pillow form. The pillow cover is lined to finish off the edges and to make it reversible. Select lightweight fabrics so the pillow cover can be gathered up tightly at the center; avoid fabrics that are stiff.

Twisted welting or fabric-covered welting is applied to the outer edge of the pillow cover. The welting defines the edge and helps the rosette stand out.

✂ Cutting Directions

For a 12" (30.5 cm) pillow, cut one 30" (76 cm) circle from the outer fabric and one from the lining. For a 14" (35.5 cm) pillow, cut 35" (89 cm) circles, or for a 16" (40.5 cm) pillow, cut 40" (102 cm) circles. To make it easier to mark and cut the circles, cut a square of each fabric, 1" (2.5 cm) larger than the diameter of the circle; then follow step 1, opposite.

Also cut a fabric strip, 2" × 18" (5 × 46 cm), to tie around the center of the pillow.

If fabric-covered welting is desired for the outer edge, cut bias fabric strips, with the combined length of the strips equal to the circumference of the circle. To estimate the length needed, multiply the diameter by three and one-half. The width of the bias strips depends on the size of the cording (page 64). For a 12" (30.5 cm) pillow, 5/32" cording works well; for a larger pillow, use 8/32" cording.

YOU WILL NEED

Decorator fabrics for outer fabric and lining.

Twisted welting with welting tape or lip; or cording and fabric for fabric-covered welting.

Circular pillow form.

How to Sew a Reversible Rosette Pillow

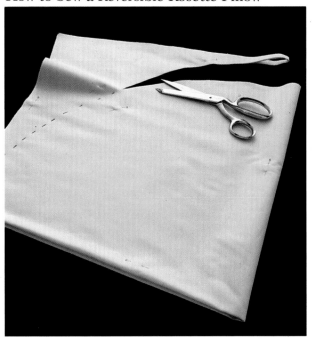

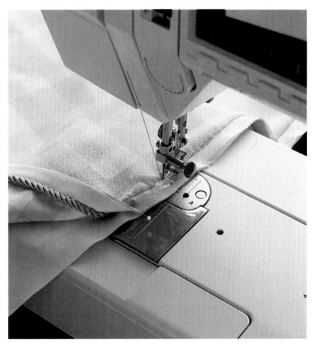

1) Fold fabric square into fourths, right sides together. Using straightedge and pencil, mark one-quarter of the circle on fabric, measuring a distance equal to the radius from the folded center of fabric. Cut on marked line through all layers; notch raw edge at foldlines. Use as pattern for cutting and notching remaining fabric circle.

2) Apply twisted welting to outer edge of one fabric circle, as on pages 68 and 69, steps 1 to 5. Or make fabric-covered welting and apply to outer edge, as on page 65, steps 1 to 5. Pin fabric circles, right sides together, matching notches; stitch close to welting, using zipper foot and leaving 6" (15 cm) opening for turning.

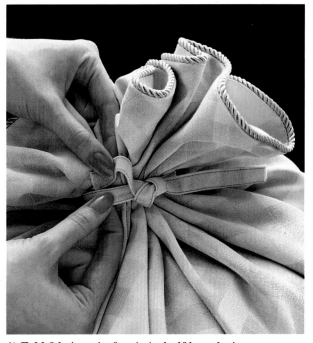

3) Turn pillow cover right side out; press. Slipstitch opening closed. Center pillow form on pillow cover; draw up fabric around pillow form, securing with rubber band. Adjust folds, arranging welting for desired effect.

4) Fold fabric strip for tie in half lengthwise, wrong sides together; press. Fold raw edges to center and press. Refold, and edgestitch on both long edges. Tie around bunched fabric, concealing rubber band and cinching in pillow cover tightly. Cut ends to desired length; tuck ends under tie to conceal them.

Sash Pillows

Sash pillows coordinate well with scarf swag window treatments and may have either a rosette or a tie at the center of the sash. The rosette can also be used at the center of the sunburst window treatment for an arch, or Palladian, window (pages 42 and 43).

✂ Cutting Directions

Cut two 17" (43 cm) squares of fabric for the pillow body and one 23" (58.5 cm) square for the sash. Cut bias strips for cording from contrasting fabric, with the total length of the strips equal to 2 yd. (1.85 m); piece the strips together as necessary. The width of the bias strips depends on the size of the cording (page 64).

For a pillow with a rosette, also cut one 25" (63.5 cm) circle for the rosette from contrasting fabric. To make it easier to mark and cut the circle, cut a 26" (66 cm) square of fabric; then follow step 1 on page 79.

For a pillow with a tie, also cut one 5" × 6" (12.5 × 15 cm) rectangle for the tie from contrasting fabric.

YOU WILL NEED

½ yd. (0.5 m) decorator fabric for pillow body.

1½ yd. (1.4 m) contrasting decorator fabric for pillow with rosette, to make rosette, sash, and bias cording.

¾ yd. (0.7 m) contrasting decorator fabric for pillow with tie, to make tie, sash, and bias cording.

2 yd. (1.85 m) cording.

Pillow form, 16" (40.5 cm).

How to Make a Rosette

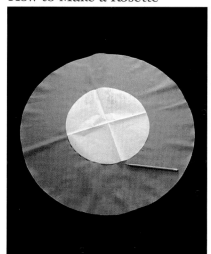

1) Mark center of rosette circle on right side of fabric, using a pencil. Make paper pattern of circle with 12" (30.5 cm) diameter; mark center. Match centers of fabric and paper circles; trace outline of paper circle onto right side of fabric.

2) Finish outer edge of circle, using zigzag or overlock stitch. Hand-baste on marked lines of small circle, using ½" (1.3 cm) running stitches. Pull basting stitches tight; secure threads. Hand-baste around outer edge and pull basting stitches tight; secure stitches, but do not cut thread tails.

3) Position eraser end of pencil on marked center of rosette. Push the center of smaller pouf through the opening at center of larger pouf; secure fabric on wrong side. Do not cut thread tails.

How to Sew a Sash Pillow with a Rosette

1) Fold 23" (58.5 cm) fabric square in half, right sides together. Stitch long edges together; press seam open. Turn tube right side out; center seam on underside of tube. Fold tube in half, matching raw edges. Press fold; do not press lengthwise edges.

2) Open out sash; hand-baste on pressed foldline. Pull basting stitches tight to cinch the sash at center.

3) Lay sash diagonally across pillow top, right sides up, pinning seams of sash at corners of pillow top. Trim excess sash fabric.

4) Make piping and apply to pillow top, as on page 65, steps 1 to 5.

5) Place the pillow back on pillow front, right sides together. Stitch around all sides of pillow close to cording, using zipper foot; leave an opening on one side for turning.

6) Turn pillow right side out. Insert pillow form. Hand-stitch rosette to sash over basting stitches. Slipstitch opening of pillow closed.

How to Sew a Sash Pillow with a Tie

1) Complete steps 1 to 5, opposite. Fold 5" × 6" (12.5 × 15 cm) rectangle of fabric in half lengthwise, right sides together. Stitch ½" (1.3 cm) seam along 6" (15 cm) side; turn right side out. Press flat, with seam centered on underside of tie.

2) Turn pillow right side out. Insert pillow form. Fold in one end of tie. Wrap tie around center of the sash, tucking raw edge into folded end; slipstitch in place. Turn tie so seam is under sash. Slipstitch opening of pillow closed.

Reversible Rolled Bolsters

The reversible rolled bolster is edged with piping to add dimension and appeal. This soft pillow is actually a fabric cover and batting rolled together for easy construction. The bolster is lined to finish off the edges and to make it reversible. The ends of the bolster are tied with bows.

The striped fabric in the pillow above has been railroaded (page 21) so the stripes encircle the bolster. Extra yardage is needed for railroading.

✂ Cutting Directions

For pillow body, cut one 18" × 45" (46 × 115 cm) rectangle of decorator fabric and one of lining. For welting, cut bias fabric strips, with combined length of strips equal to 3¼ yd. (3 m). The width of the bias strips depends on the size of the cording (page 64). For ties, cut two 1½" × 28" (3.8 × 71 cm) fabric strips.

Cut as many 12" × 30" (30.5 × 76 cm) rectangles of batting as necessary for 2" to 3" (5 to 7.5 cm) thickness.

YOU WILL NEED

½ yd. (0.5 m) decorator fabric for pillow body, or 1¼ yd. (1.15 m) if fabric is to be railroaded.

½ yd. (0.5 m) contrasting fabric for lining.

¾ yd. (0.7 m) matching or contrasting fabric for ties and welting.

3¼ yd. (3 m) cording.

Quilt batting.

How to Sew a Rolled Bolster

1) Round corners at one short end of rectangle. Make welting as on page 65, step 1. Machine-baste welting on right side of one fabric piece to long sides and rounded end, matching raw edges and stitching over previous stitches; ease cording at corners and leave at least 3" (7.5 cm) of welting at ends.

2) Remove stitching from ends of welting. Trim cords ½" (1.3 cm) from raw edges of pillow fabric. Fold excess fabric strip back over welting, then diagonally, as shown. Pin, and stitch in place.

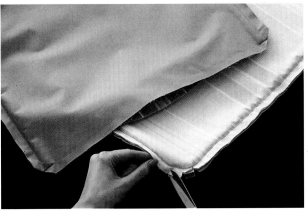

3) Pin fabric pieces, right sides together. Stitch on all sides, stitching as close as possible to welting; leave 6" (15 cm) opening at the end without welting. Notch out rounded corners to remove excess fullness. Turn right side out; press. Stitch opening closed.

4) Fold each tie in half lengthwise, right sides together; stitch ¼" (6 mm) seam on long edge. Turn ties right side out, using loop turner; tuck in and slipstitch ends.

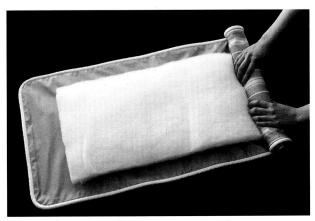

5) Center batting on finished rectangle. Roll fabric up to batting, starting from the end without welting.

6) Continue rolling fabric and batting together loosely. Tie ends tightly. Shape welting at ends for spiral effect.

Sewing for the Bedroom

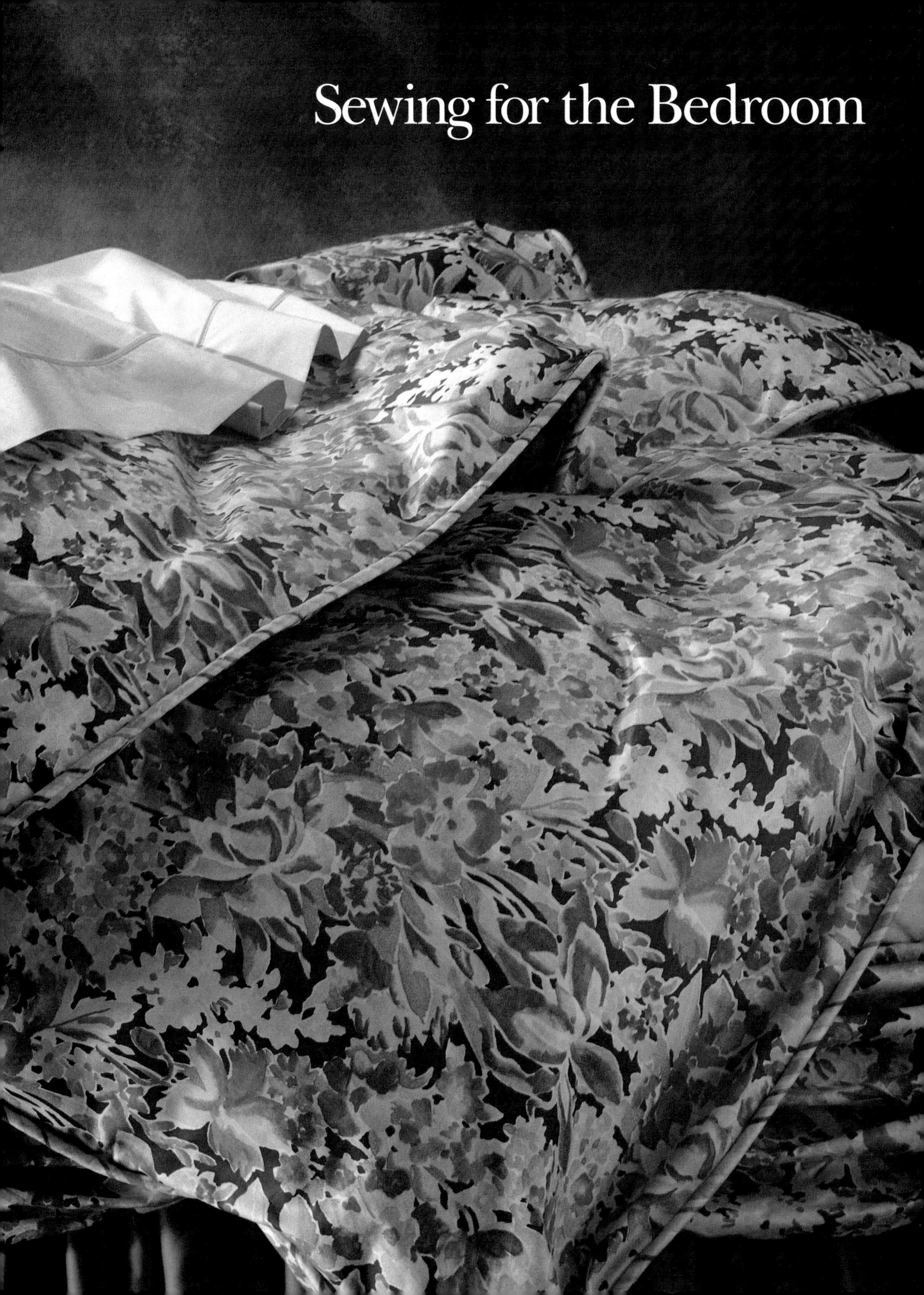

Envelope Pillow Shams

These pillow shams open like an envelope, making it easy to insert pillows; the flap closes with hook and loop tape. Edged in plain or gathered jumbo welting, these pillows can be either traditional or contemporary. Make envelope pillow shams for any size bed pillow.

✂ Cutting Directions

Cut one rectangle of fabric for the pillow back/flap. The cut width is equal to the pillow width plus 1" (2.5 cm) for seam allowances; cut length is equal to one and two-thirds of the pillow length plus 1" (2.5 cm) for seam allowances.

Cut one rectangle of fabric for the pillow front. The cut width is equal to the pillow width plus 1" (2.5 cm) for seam allowances; cut length is equal to the pillow length plus 2" (5 cm) for seam and hem allowances.

Cut one rectangle of fabric for the flap facing. The cut width is equal to the pillow width plus 1" (2.5 cm) for seam allowances; cut length is equal to two-thirds of the pillow length plus 5" (12.5 cm) for overlap.

Cut fabric strips for plain jumbo welting (page 64) or gathered jumbo welting (page 66).

YOU WILL NEED

Decorator fabric for pillow.

Decorator fabric for welting. Allow up to ½ yd. (0.5 m) for plain jumbo welting, 1 yd. (0.95 m) for double-fullness gathered jumbo welting, or 1½ yd. (1.4 m) for triple-fullness gathered jumbo welting. Exact yardage depends on width of fabric, sizes of cording and pillow, and fullness of welting.

Jumbo cording, equal to the distance around the pillow back/flap.

1" (2.5 cm) hook and loop tape for closure.

How to Sew an Envelope Sham

1) Fold the pillow back/flap and flap facing in half lengthwise; mark end of flap 4" (10 cm) from fold for bed pillow or 3" (7.5 cm) from fold for accent pillow. Mark two-thirds the length of pillow on the edge opposite fold. Draw diagonal line between marks; cut on marked line. Round corners of flap and lower edges of pillow front and pillow back/flap.

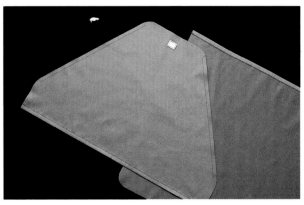

2) Press under ½" (1.3 cm) twice on one crosswise edge of pillow front and on long crosswise edge of flap facing; stitch to make double-fold hems. Stitch loop side of hook and loop tape to flap facing, centered about 1" (2.5 cm) from short edge. Staystitch bias edges of flap and flap facing.

3) Place pillow front over pillow back/flap, right sides together, matching raw edges. Place flap facing over flap portion of pillow back/flap, right sides together, matching raw edges. Pin pillow front and flap facing together in lapped area; stitch a rectangle 2" × ½" (5 × 1.3 cm) at ends of overlap.

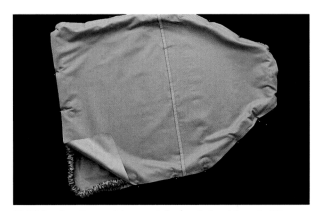

4) Make jumbo welting; apply to right side of pillow back/flap. Follow steps 1 to 7 on pages 66 and 67 for gathered welting, or steps 1 to 5 on page 65 for plain welting. Place pillow front/flap facing on pillow back/flap, right sides together; pin.

5) Stitch around pillow sham through all layers, using zipper foot; stitch inside previous stitching line. Finish seam allowances, using overlock stitch on serger or zigzag stitch on conventional machine.

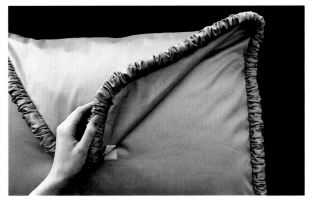

6) Turn sham right side out; insert pillow. Pin hook side of hook and loop tape in position, under flap, on pillow front. Remove pillow and stitch tape in place.

Duvet Covers

Duvet covers can protect a new comforter or change the look of an existing one. Less bulky to handle than a full-size bedspread, a duvet cover is as easy to sew as a pillow sham. For a complete bed set, make the duvet cover, bed skirt, and pillow shams to coordinate.

The drop length of the duvet cover must be long enough to extend beyond the upper edge of the bed skirt and cover any blankets. The drop length is usually about 3" (7.5 cm) longer than the depth of the mattress. Purchased comforters may vary in drop length from 9" to 14" (23 to 35.5 cm). If the drop length is too short, jumbo welting or a ruffle can be added to the duvet cover.

To determine how many widths of fabric are needed, divide the total width of the duvet cover by the fabric width; round off to the next highest number. Most duvet covers require two fabric widths. Multiply the number of widths by the length of the duvet cover for the amount of fabric needed. Divide by 36" (100 cm) to determine the number of yards (meters).

✂ Cutting Directions

Determine the finished size of the duvet cover by measuring the size of the comforter. The finished

duvet cover may be the same size as the comforter, or, for a snug fit on a down comforter, the duvet cover may be up to 2" (5 cm) shorter and narrower than the comforter.

The cut size of the duvet front is 1" (2.5 cm) wider and longer than the finished size. When more than one fabric width is required, cut one full width for the center panel of the duvet cover and two equal, partial-width panels for each side; add an extra ½" (1.3 cm) seam allowance to each panel for seaming them together. Cut the duvet back the same width as the duvet front, and 1½" (3.8 cm) shorter than the front. Cut a zipper strip 3½" (9 cm) wide and the same length as the cut width of the duvet back.

Cut fabric strips for plain jumbo welting (page 64), gathered jumbo welting (page 66), or ruffle (page 76).

YOU WILL NEED

Decorator fabric.

Two zippers, each 22" (56 cm) long.

Welting or ruffle, optional.

How to Sew a Duvet Cover

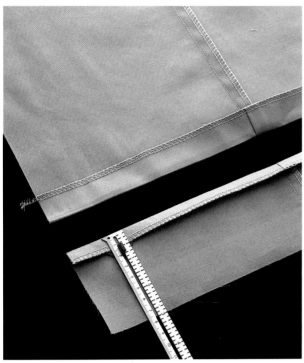

1) **Overlock** or zigzag upper edge of zipper strip and lower edge of duvet back. Press the finished edge of zipper strip under ½" (1.3 cm) and the finished edge of back under 1" (2.5 cm).

2) **Place** closed zippers face down on seam allowance of duvet back, with zipper tabs meeting in center and with edges of zipper tapes on fold. Using zipper foot, stitch along one side of zippers.

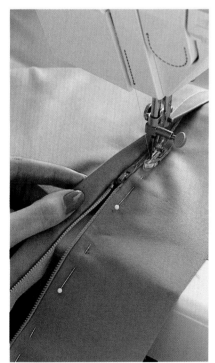

3) **Turn** right side up. Pin pressed edge of zipper strip along edge of zipper teeth; stitch close to pressed edge. Backstitch at ends of zippers.

4) **Stitch** across end of one zipper; then topstitch through all layers to stitch seam from zipper to side of duvet cover. Repeat at other end of zipper. Open zippers. (Contrasting thread was used to show detail.)

5) **Apply** welting, if desired, and stitch duvet front to duvet back as for pillows (page 65). Turn duvet cover right side out; insert duvet.

Ideas for Duvet Covers

Make a duvet cover to coordinate with pillow shams and other room accessories. Because the construction of duvet covers is similar to that of pillow covers, most pillow designs can be adapted to make coordinating duvet covers.

Twisted welting and a coordinating ruffle have been added to this duvet cover, using the same basic construction as the sunburst pillow (page 76). The ruffle and the twisted welting are applied to the sides and the lower edge of the duvet back after the zipper is inserted; the upper edge is not ruffled.

Bows or rosettes can be tied at the corners of a duvet cover for an added detail that coordinates with bow picture hangers (page 102) or sash pillows (page 80).

Knotted jumbo welting is added to this duvet cover to coordinate with the knotted-corner pillows (page 72). The jumbo welting is inserted into fabric sleeves on three sides of the duvet cover; the upper edge of the duvet cover does not have welting.

Circular Ruffle Bed Skirt

The circular ruffle bed skirt has soft draping. Its simple style complements a tailored decor, but also works well for a room that is elaborately decorated, without detracting from other furnishings.

The circular ruffle bed skirt is easy to sew and requires less time than most bed skirts, because there are no gathers or pleats. To prevent the bed skirt from shifting out of position, the upper edge of the skirt is attached to a fitted sheet. If the bed does not have a footboard, the bed skirt is attached as one continuous strip. For a bed with a footboard, a split-corner bed skirt can be attached to the sheet in three sections.

✂ Cutting Directions

Determine the number of circular pieces required, as indicated in the chart, opposite. To make it easier to cut the circles, cut fabric squares the size of the circle diameter; then cut the circular pieces, opposite.

The calculations given in the chart are based on a 15½" (39.3 cm) cut length. This gives an adequate amount of ruffling for any cut length up to at least 15½" (39.3 cm); you may have excess ruffling, which can easily be cut off during construction. The actual length of ruffling per circle is equal to the circumference of the inner circle minus 1" (2.5 cm) for seams and side hems.

YOU WILL NEED

Decorator fabric, in the yardage amount indicated in the chart, opposite.

Fitted sheet.

How to Cut Circles

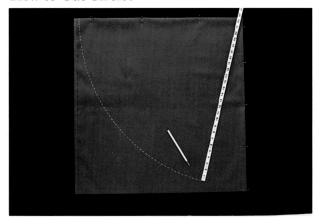

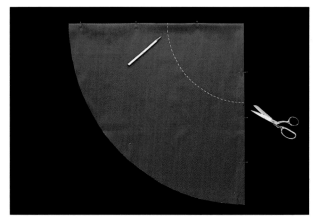

1) Fold the fabric square in half lengthwise, then crosswise, right sides together. Using straightedge and pencil, mark an arc on fabric, measuring from the folded center of fabric, a distance equal to the radius. Cut on marked line through all layers.

2) Add 1" (2.5 cm) to the drop length of bed skirt; measure and mark this distance away from arc. Draw second arc at this distance. Cut on marked line through all layers. Circumference of inner circle minus 1" (2.5 cm) determines length of ruffling per circle.

How to Cut Half-circles

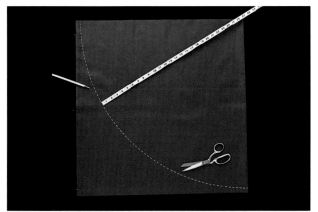

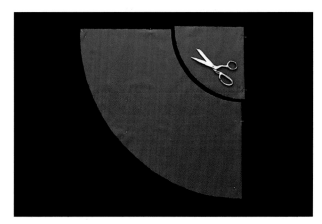

1) Cut rectangle across the width of fabric, with short sides equal to one-half the width of the fabric. Fold fabric in half, matching short sides. Using straightedge and pencil, mark an arc on fabric, measuring from the lengthwise fold, a distance equal to the radius. Cut on marked line through both layers.

2) Add 1" (2.5 cm) to the drop length of bed skirt; measure and mark this distance away from arc. Draw second arc at this distance. Cut on marked line through both layers.

Determining the Circular Pieces Needed

Diameter of Circles	Ruffling Length per Circle	Twin		Full		Queen		King	
		Circles Needed	Yardage Needed	Circles Needed	Yardage Needed	Circles Needed	Yardage Needed	Circles Needed	Yardage Needed
45" (115 cm)	47" (120 cm)	4	5 yd. (4.6 m)	4½	5⅝ yd. (5.15 m)	5	6¼ yd. (5.75 m)	5½	6⅞ yd. (6.3 m)
48" (122 cm)	58" (147 cm)	3½	4⅔ yd. (4.33 m)	3½	4⅔ yd. (4.33 m)	4	5⅓ yd. (4.92 m)	4½	6 yd. (5.5 m)
54" (137 cm)	76" (193 cm)	2½	3¾ yd. (3.45 m)	3	4½ yd. (4.15 m)	3	4½ yd. (4.15 m)	3½	5¼ yd. (4.8 m)
60" (153 cm)	95" (242 cm)	2	3⅓ yd. (3.07 m)	2½	4¼ yd. (3.9 m)	2½	4¼ yd. (3.9 m)	3	5 yd. (4.6 m)

How to Sew a Circular Ruffle Bed Skirt

1) Cut circles for bed skirt (pages 94 and 95). Slash each piece from outer to inner edges on crosswise grain. Staystitch ½" (1.3 cm) from inner edge.

2) Stitch circles together in a long strip, right sides together; finish seam allowances. Clip up to the staystitching at 2" (5 cm) intervals; space the clips evenly so bed skirt will hang in even folds.

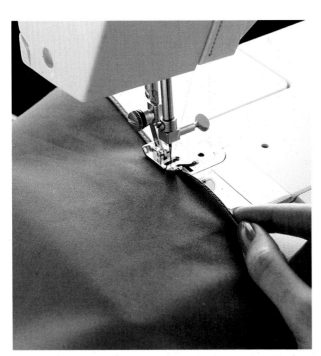

3) Machine-stitch ¼" (6 mm) from hem edge. Turn edge to wrong side on stitching line; press fold. Stitch close to fold. Trim excess fabric close to stitching. Turn hem edge to wrong side a scant ¼" (6 mm), enclosing raw edge. Edgestitch.

4) Place fitted sheet over box spring; mark sheet along upper edge of box spring, using water-soluble marking pen or chalk.

5) Lay circular ruffle on top of box spring; pin ruffle to sheet, right sides together, matching staystitching to marked line. Ruffle may extend around corners at head of bed, if desired; extend raw edge ½" (1.3 cm) beyond desired endpoint to allow for side hem.

6) Mark side hems at head of bed perpendicular to floor, allowing ½" (1.3 cm) for double ¼" (6 mm) hem.

7) Remove fitted sheet and ruffle from bed. Cut off any excess ruffle at sides; stitch side hems. Stitch ruffle to fitted sheet, stitching just beyond staystitching.

Split corners. Follow steps 1 to 4. Cut ruffle into three sections, each section long enough to fit on one side of the bed plus 1" (2.5 cm) for side hems. Lay section for foot of bed on top of box spring; pin to sheet, right sides together, matching staystitching to marked line. Mark side hems at corner, as in step 6. Pin side sections to sheet, overlapping hem allowances at corners. Complete bed skirt, as in steps 6 and 7.

Swag Bed Skirt

The swag bed skirt has soft drapes of fabric that are layered over a gathered underskirt. This treatment complements swag window treatments and works well for bedrooms with romantic, feminine styling. To show off the bed skirt to its best advantage, select a duvet cover with a drop length that is only 1" to 2" (2.5 to 5 cm) below the mattress.

For easier draping of the swags, two-cord shirring tape is used. For a more finished look, matching or contrasting straps are added to cover the shirring tape. The entire bed skirt is attached to a fitted sheet, which prevents the skirt from shifting out of position.

For a bed with a footboard, a split-corner underskirt can be sewn by attaching three sections to the fitted sheet. For this style, the three sections are hemmed at both sides, and the sections are butted together at the corner. If the bed does not have a footboard, the underskirt is sewn in one continuous strip.

✂ Cutting Directions

Determine the number of swags you will need for the bed skirt, according to the chart, opposite. The size of the swags will vary, depending on the size of the bed. Also, the swags will be a slightly different size on the foot of the bed than on the sides, but this difference is unnoticeable.

Cut a rectangle of fabric for each swag; railroad the fabric to avoid seaming, or piece the rectangles, as necessary. Cut the rectangles 27" (68.5 cm) long and 5" (12.5 cm) wider than the distance between the markings in step 1, on page 100. If you are using a patterned fabric with large motifs, you may want to center a motif on each rectangle.

Cut 3" × 11" (7.5 × 28 cm) straps from matching or contrasting fabric. You will need one strap for each swag plus one extra strap.

For a bed without a footboard, the cut width of the gathered underskirt is two and one-half to three times the distance around the sides and foot of the bed; the fabric may be railroaded or fabric widths may be pieced together, as necessary. The cut length of the underskirt is equal to the distance from the top of the box spring to the floor plus 2" (5 cm). This allows for the hem and seam allowances and for ½" (1.3 cm) clearance at the floor.

For a bed with a footboard, make a split-corner underskirt. The cut width for each of the two side sections is two and one-half to three times the length of the bed, and the cut width for the foot section is two and one-half to three times the width of the bed. The cut length of the sections is equal to the distance from the top of the box spring to the floor plus 2" (5 cm).

YOU WILL NEED

Decorator fabric.

Fitted sheet.

Two-cord shirring tape, 23½" (59.8 cm) for each swag plus an extra 23½" (59.8 cm).

Determining the Number of Swags Needed

No. of Swags	Twin	Full	Queen	King
At foot	1	2	2	3
Each side	2	3	3	3
Total swags	5	8	8	9

How to Sew a Swag Bed Skirt

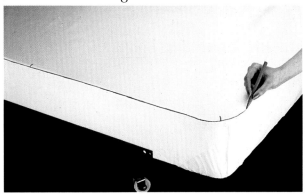

1) Place fitted sheet over box spring; mark sheet along upper edge of box spring, using water-soluble marking pen or chalk. Mark corners at upper edge of box spring on sheet at center of curve. Divide each side of bed into equal parts according to the number of swags.

2) Fold each rectangle in half crosswise; measure and mark 2" (5 cm) in from corner along upper edge. Draw line diagonally to opposite corner. Cut on marked line through both layers.

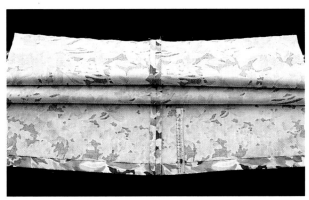

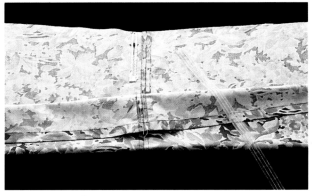

3) Press and stitch 1" (2.5 cm) double-fold hem at lower edge of each swag piece. Stitch swag pieces together; press seams open. Press under ½" (1.3 cm) at the sides.

4) Fold under ½" (1.3 cm) on both ends of shirring tape. Center tape over one seam on wrong side, starting above hem; pin in place. Stitch three rows of stitching on tape; stitch along center first, then along outer edges. Repeat for remaining seams and at sides.

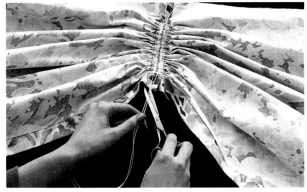

5) Knot cords at upper end of tape. Pull cords from lower end, gathering fabric as tightly as possible; knot ends securely. Trim tails.

6) Fold strap pieces in half lengthwise, right sides together; stitch ¼" (6 mm) seam. Turn straps right side out; press. Pin straps to fitted sheet, centering them over markings; extend ½" (1.3 cm) at end of each strap beyond marked line, as shown.

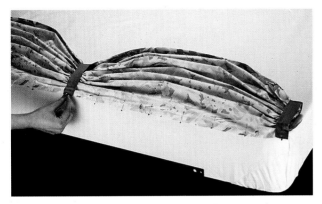

7) Lay swags on top of box spring; pin upper edge to sheet, right sides together, extending ½" (1.3 cm) seam allowance beyond marked line. Wrap straps around swags; pin in place, matching ends. If desired, remove sheet from bed and machine-baste upper edge of swags in place, stitching scant ½" (1.3 cm) from raw edge.

8) Seam underskirt panels together; for bed without footboard, stitch panels in one continuous strip, or for bed with footboard, stitch panels in three sections. Finish seam allowances. Press and stitch 1" (2.5 cm) double-fold hem at lower edge of underskirt. Stitch ½" (1.3 cm) double-fold side hems.

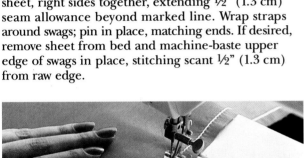

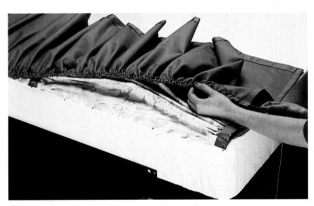

9) Zigzag over a cord at upper edge of underskirt, within seam allowance, just beyond seamline. Zigzag over second cord ¼" (6 mm) from first cord, if desired, for more control when adjusting gathers.

10) Divide marked line on fitted sheet and upper edge of underskirt into fourths or eighths. Lay underskirt, right side down, over swags; match and pin together at markings. Pull on gathering cords, and gather underskirt evenly to fit; pin.

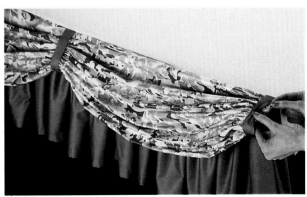

11) Remove bed skirt and sheet from bed. Stitch bed skirt to sheet, stitching ½" (1.3 cm) from raw edge.

12) Place bed skirt on box spring. Hand-stitch straps to swags at head of bed. Arrange folds of swags.

Bow
Picture Hangers

These attractive bows are used to accent a painting or portrait. They add interest to the wall at a higher level than most room furnishings, and they draw the eye upward, visually adding height to a room. Originally used to support the weight of pictures, bow picture hangers are now used as decorative, nonfunctional accessories.

Bow picture hangers are an excellent use for the long, narrow side cuts of fabric that are frequently left over after sewing other projects. For best results, use a fabric that has body, so the bow will hold its shape. Chintz and moiré are frequently used for crisp bows.

Bow picture hangers can be made to any size. The instructions that follow are for a picture hanger about 50" (127 cm) long.

✂ Cutting Directions
Cut one 11" × 34" (28 × 86.5 cm) piece of decorator fabric for bow, two 7" × 54" (18 × 137 cm) pieces for tails, and two 3" × 5" (7.5 × 12.5 cm) pieces for ties. These measurements include ½" (1.3 cm) seam allowances.

YOU WILL NEED

Decorator fabric.

Small plastic curtain ring.

How to Sew a Bow Picture Hanger

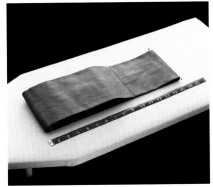

1) Fold bow piece in half lengthwise, right sides together; stitch long edges. Press seam open. Turn right side out. Press, centering seam on back of bow.

2) Stitch short ends, right sides together. Turn right side out. Fold in half, with seam at one end; pin-mark foldline. Stitch across the width of the bow, through all layers, 10" (25.5 cm) from seam.

3) Flatten bow, with stitching lines and marked foldline in the middle of the bow. Stitch through all layers at middle.

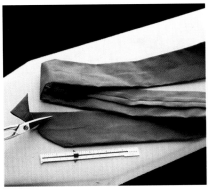

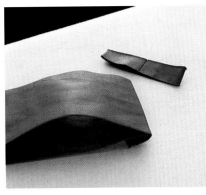

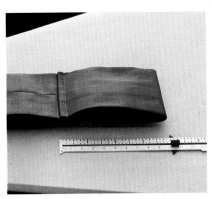

4) Stitch long edges of each tail, right sides together; press seam open. Center seam on back; mark points 2" (5 cm) up from lower edge at sides. Draw lines from marks to ½" (1.3 cm) from raw edge at the center. Stitch on marked lines; trim excess fabric.

5) Turn tails right side out; press, centering seams on back. Press under ¾" (2 cm) at upper edge of one tail; trim ¾" (2 cm) from remaining tail. With right sides up, place tails together as shown.

6) Fold both tails over 4" (10 cm) from fold at upper edge. Stitch through all layers ¼" (6 mm) from first fold.

7) Fold in raw edges of tie pieces to make ties 1¼" × 5" (3.2 × 12.5 cm); press. Pinch bow at center. Hand-stitch one tie over center of bow, turning under raw edge.

8) Pull remaining tie through the previous tie. Pinch tails 4" (10 cm) from upper edge. Hand-stitch tie around tails, turning under raw edge.

9) Stitch curtain ring on back of bow for hanging on wall.

Slipcovers

Slipcovers

Slipcovers are removable covers, positioned over the existing fabric of the furniture. They can extend the life of a piece of furniture and update the decor at the same time. You can even change the look in a room from season to season by changing slipcovers. Because the pattern is developed when the first slipcover is made for the piece of furniture, a second slipcover can be made in less time.

A frequent concern about a slipcover is whether it will stay in place. To help secure the slipcover, an attached fabric strip, concealed under the skirt, is pinned to the existing fabric. Also, polyurethane foam pieces are tucked along the sides of the deck to provide a tight fit.

Sewing slipcovers is an alternative to upholstering. However, upholstering is required when the furniture needs structural repair, such as springing. It is easier to sew slipcovers for furniture that is fairly square, with straight lines, than it is for furniture with more details. Furniture with exposed wood usually requires upholstering, but furniture with wood strips on the arm can be slipcovered if the arms are first wrapped with upholstery batting. Recliners should be upholstered because of the movable parts.

Furniture with a concave back design, such as a channel back or barrel back, is difficult to slipcover, and the slipcover may not fit well. For best results, a concave back should be wrapped or covered in a thick upholstery batting before it is slipcovered. Furniture with a tufted back or button back can be slipcovered, but the tufting and buttons are eliminated in the slipcover. The back is wrapped with upholstery batting to fill it out for a smooth-fitting slipcover.

Selecting the Slipcover Fabric

Decorator fabrics are recommended for slipcovers. Heavy upholstery fabrics should be avoided, because they are difficult to sew on most home sewing machines and do not shape easily around curves. Regardless of the fabric selection, dry cleaning is recommended instead of washing to keep the slipcover looking its best.

It may be necessary to underline the slipcover if the fabric on the furniture is heavily textured and the slipcover fabric is smooth, or if the fabric on the furniture is dark or bright and the slipcover fabric is light-colored.

For faster and easier sewing, select a fabric that does not require matching, such as solid-colored fabrics or allover prints. Striped fabrics require matching in one direction, and plaids require matching in both directions. Many print fabrics have a 27" (68.5 cm) pattern repeat, which fits perfectly on most cushions.

The amount of fabric required depends on the size of the furniture, pattern pieces, fabric width, and pattern repeat. Depending on how close together the pattern pieces can be cut, there may be a lot of scraps. Frequently these scraps can be used for room accessories, such as pillows and bow picture hangers.

As a general rule, a chair requires about 7 to 8 yd. (6.4 to 7.35 m); a love seat, 10 to 12 yd. (9.15 to 11 m); and a sofa, 16 to 20 yd. (14.7 to 19.4 m). These amounts include matching welting and a skirt with pleats at the corners. Allow additional fabric for cushions and ruffled or box-pleated skirts. Each cushion requires 1 to 1½ yd. (0.95 to 1.4 m) of fabric. For a ruffled or box-pleated skirt, allow 1 yd. (0.95 m) extra for a chair, 2 to 3 yd. (1.85 to 2.75 m) for a love seat, and 4 yd. (3.7 m) for a sofa.

YOU WILL NEED

Muslin for pin-fitting the pieces.

Decorator fabric.

Cording for welting; select soft, pliable cording with a cotton core.

Zippers; one for chairs, two for sofas and love seats. The length of each zipper is 1" to 2" (2.5 to 5 cm) shorter than the length of the vertical seam at the side of the outside back. Additional zippers are needed for cushions (page 122).

Upholstery batting, if necessary, to pad the existing furniture.

Polyurethane foam, 2" (5 cm) strips, to insert at sides and back of deck.

T-pins, tacks, or heavy-duty stapler and staples, for securing tacking strip to furniture.

Pin-fitting

The easiest way to make a slipcover pattern is by pin-fitting muslin on the chair or sofa. Before you start, look carefully at the furniture. Usually the seams in the slipcover will be in the same locations as the seams on the existing cover, but you may be able to add or eliminate some details, provided it will not affect the fit of the slipcover. For example, if the existing cushions are wrap-style, you may want to slipcover them as box cushions with welting. Or a chair with a pleated front arm may be slipcovered with a separate front arm piece.

The style of the skirt can also be changed. You may want to gather a skirt all the way around the furniture, allowing double fullness. Or you may want bunched gathers at the corners of a chair, or at the corners and center front of a sofa. For a more tailored look, the skirt may have box pleats instead of gathers.

A chair with rolled arms and loose back and seat cushions is used in the instructions that follow. This example includes the details that are common to most furniture. Although your furniture style may be somewhat different, use these basic steps as a guide.

How to Pin-fit the Pattern for the Inside Back and Outside Back

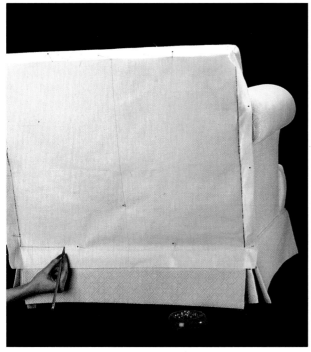

1) Remove cushions. Measure outside back of chair or sofa between seamlines; cut muslin 3" to 4" (7.5 to 10 cm) larger than measurements. Mark center line on outside back piece, following lengthwise grain. Pin to chair, smoothing fabric; mark seamlines.

2) Measure inside back between seamlines; cut muslin 15" (38 cm) wider and about 10" (25.5 cm) longer than measurements. This allows for 6" (15 cm) at the lower edge to tuck into the deck and hold the slipcover in place. Mark center line on inside back piece, following lengthwise grain.

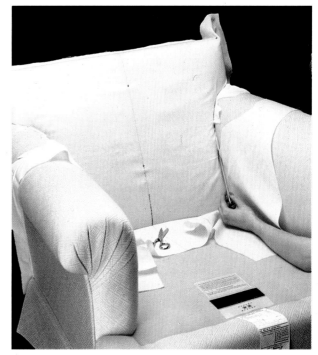

3) Pin outside back and inside back together along top of chair or sofa, matching center lines. Fold out excess fabric on inside back piece at upper corner, forming a dart. Pin muslin snugly, but do not pull fabric tight.

4) Trim excess fabric on sides of inside back to 2" (5 cm); clip along arms as necessary for smooth curve. Push about ½" (1.3 cm) of fabric into crevices on sides and lower edge of inside back; mark seamlines by pushing pencil into crevices.

How to Pin-fit the Pattern for a Pleated Arm

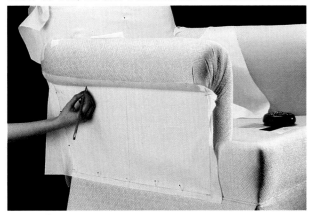

1) Measure outside arm between seamlines; cut muslin 3" (7.5 cm) larger than measurements. Mark lengthwise grainline on muslin. Pin outside arm in place, with grainline perpendicular to floor and with lower edge extending ½" (1.3 cm) beyond seamline at upper edge of skirt. Smooth fabric upward; pin. Pin outside arm to outside back. Mark seamlines.

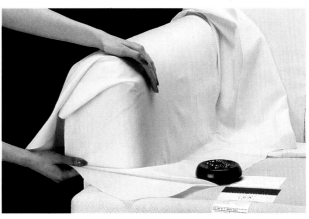

2) Measure inside arm from deck to seamline at upper edge of outside arm, and from inside back to front of arm; cut muslin about 9" (23 cm) larger than measurements. Mark lengthwise grainline on muslin. Pin inside arm piece in place, with 7" (18 cm) extending at inside back and grainline straight across arm, smoothing fabric up and around arm.

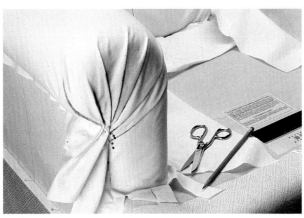

3) Pin inside arm to outside arm at front; clip and trim fabric at front lower edge as necessary for smooth fit. Pleat out fabric for rolled arm to duplicate pleats in existing fabric. Mark radiating foldlines of pleats.

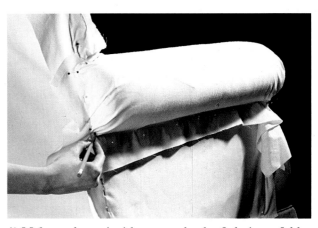

4) Make tucks on inside arm at back of chair, to fold out excess fabric; clip inside arm as necessary for smooth fit. Mark seamline at beginning and end of tucks on inside arm and outside back.

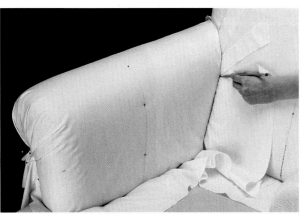

5) Mark inside arm and inside back with large dots, about halfway up the arm. Push about ½" (1.3 cm) of fabric on inside arm into crevices at deck and back.

6) Mark all seamlines on muslin, smoothing the fabric as you go.

How to Pin-fit the Pattern for an Arm with a Front Section

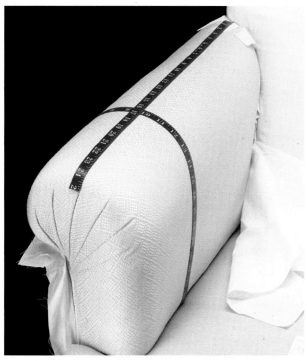

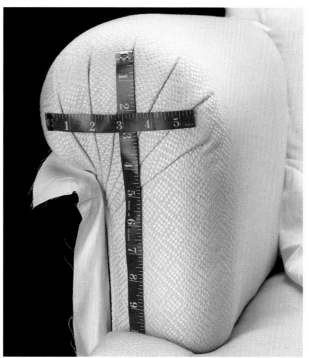

1) **Follow** step 1, opposite, for outside arm. Measure inside arm from deck to seamline at upper edge of outside arm, and from inside back to front edge of arm; cut muslin about 9" (23 cm) larger than these measurements. Mark lengthwise grainline on muslin.

2) **Measure** front of the arm; cut muslin 2" to 3" (5 to 7.5 cm) larger than measurements. Mark lengthwise grainline on muslin.

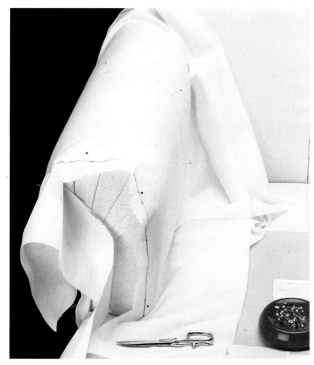

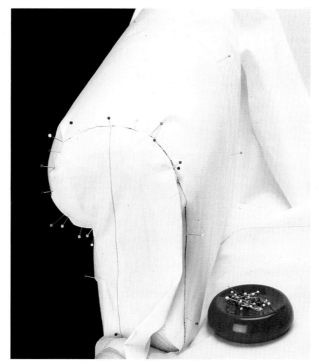

3) **Pin** inside arm piece in place, with 7" (18 cm) extending at inside back and grainline straight across arm, smoothing fabric up and around arm. Mark seamline at front edge of arm; trim away excess fabric not needed for seam allowances.

4) **Pin** front arm piece in place. Fold out excess fabric on inside arm as necessary to fit front arm piece, making two pleats. Mark seamline for curve of arm, following existing seamline on chair. Complete pattern as in steps 4, 5, and 6, opposite.

How to Pin-fit the Pattern for the Deck

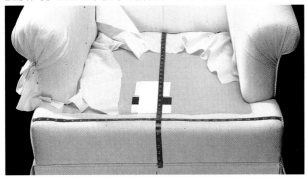

1) Measure width at front of deck; measure length of deck, down front of chair to skirt seam; cut muslin 15" (38 cm) wider and 9" (23 cm) longer than the measurements. Mark center line on muslin, following grainline. Mark seamline on muslin at front edge on straight of grain, ½" (1.3 cm) from raw edge.

2) Pin marked line on muslin to welting of skirt seam, with center line centered on skirt; this positions muslin on straight of grain. Smooth muslin over front edge and deck, and match center lines of deck and back.

3) Mark deck and inside arm pieces with large dots, at point where deck meets front of inside arm. For furniture with T-cushion, clip excess deck fabric to dot. Fold out excess fabric on deck at front corner, forming a dart; pin and mark.

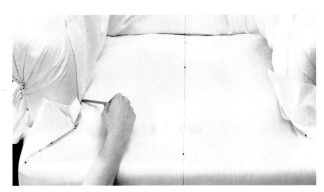

4) Pin deck to outside arm piece at side of chair; mark seamline. Do not fit deck snug. Push about ½" (1.3 cm) of fabric into crevices at sides and back of deck; mark seamlines by pushing pencil into crevices.

How to Pin-fit the Skirt

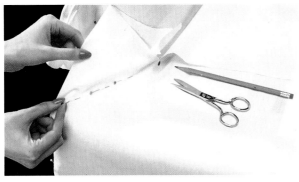

1) Measure for skirt around sides, front, and back to determine cut width of skirt; allow for gathers or pleats. Plan seam placement, based on width of fabric and size of furniture, so seams are concealed in gathers or pleats whenever possible; plan a seam at back corner where zipper will be inserted. Cut number of fabric widths needed; cut muslin pieces 1" (2.5 cm) longer than length of skirt.

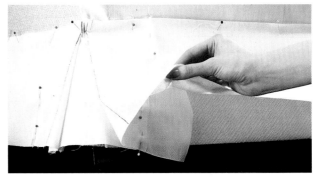

2) Place raw edge of muslin just below lower edge of skirt; pin at upper edge of skirt, keeping muslin straight and even. Pin seams as you come to them; pin out fullness for pleats or gathers. Pin vertical tucks in skirt, pinning ⅛" (3 mm) tuck near back corner on each side of chair and ¼" (6 mm) tuck near each corner on back of chair; tucks will be released in step 3, opposite, adding ease to skirt. Mark seams and placement of pleats or gathers.

How to Prepare the Pattern for Cutting

1) Mark upper edge of all muslin pieces; label pieces. Check that all seamlines, darts, gathers, and pleats are marked. Mark dots at intersecting seams; label.

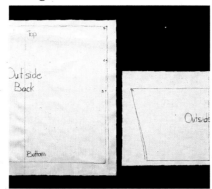

2) Remove muslin. Add ¼" (6 mm) ease to back edge of outside arm at lower corner. Add ½" (1.3 cm) ease to sides of outside back at lower corners. Taper to marked seamlines at upper corners.

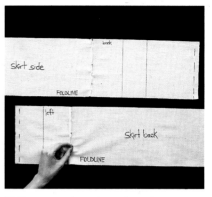

3) Remove the pinned tucks near back corners of skirt pieces. Mark "foldline" at lower edge of muslin for self-lined skirt.

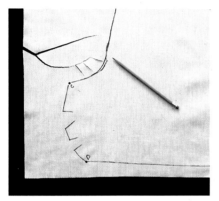

4) True straight seamlines, using straightedge; true curved seamlines, drawing smooth curves. Do not mark seamlines in pleated areas.

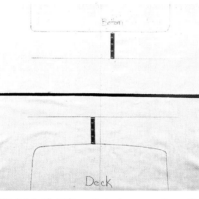

5) Add 4" (10 cm) to lower edge of inside back and back edge of deck.

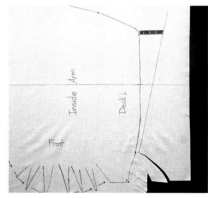

6) Mark the lower edge of inside arm from a point 4" (10 cm) away from seamline at back edge to ½" (1.3 cm) from large dot at front edge; repeat for sides of deck.

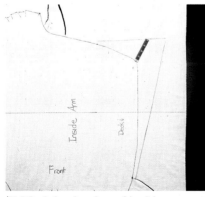

7) Mark back edge of inside arm from a point 4" (10 cm) away from seamline at the lower edge to ½" (1.3 cm) from large dot; repeat for sides of inside back.

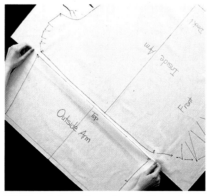

8) Check lengths of seamlines for adjoining seams; adjust as necessary to ensure that seamlines match.

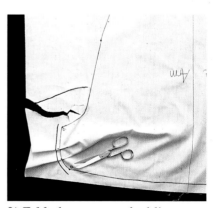

9) Fold pleats on marked lines. Mark seamlines in pleated area; add ½" (1.3 cm) seam allowances. Trim on cutting line through all layers of pleats. Add ½" (1.3 cm) seam allowances to any remaining seams. Cut pieces on marked lines.

Laying Out &
Cutting the Fabric

Whenever possible, lay out all the pattern pieces on the fabric before you start to cut. This allows you to rearrange the pieces as necessary to make the best use of the fabric. For boxed cushions, follow the cutting directions on pages 122 and 123.

When a patterned fabric with an allover design is used for slipcovers, little or no matching is required. If a patterned fabric with a one-way design is used, be careful to lay the pieces in the correct direction on the fabric. Patterned fabrics may be matched at the seamline on the upper edge of the skirt, if desired, following the technique for boxed cushions (page 125).

Center large motifs in a print fabric on the top and the bottom of the cushion. For best results, also align the design so it continues down the back of the furniture, onto the cushion, and down the skirt.

In addition to the pieces cut from the muslin pattern, you will need a 3" (7.5 cm) tacking strip cut on the straight of grain. This strip is used to secure the slipcover to the furniture with T-pins, tacks, or staples. Cut the length of the tacking strip equal to the distance around the furniture at the upper edge of the skirt.

Cut fabric strips for the welting as on page 64. Measure the seamlines that will have welting to determine the total length of the bias strips you will need to cut.

Tips for Laying Out and Cutting the Slipcover Fabric

Center large motifs, such as floral clusters, on the back, sides, cushions, and on the top of the arms.

Center the prominent stripe of a striped fabric on the center placement line of the outside and inside back pieces and on the cushion pieces. Decide in which direction the stripes will run on the arms; usually it is preferable to have the stripes run in the same direction as the stripes on the skirt.

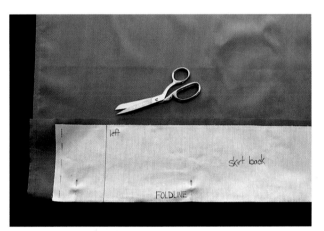

Cut the skirt pieces for a self-lined skirt, placing the foldline at lower edge of skirt on a crosswise fold of the fabric. Self-lined skirts hang better than single-layer skirts with a hem.

Cut arm pieces, right sides together, using the first piece as the pattern for cutting the second piece.

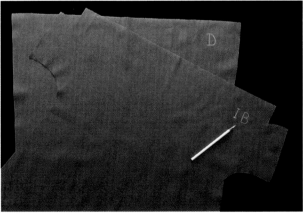

Mark names of pieces on wrong side of fabric, using chalk. Abbreviations like "D" for deck, "IB" for inside back, and "OA" for outside arm may be used.

Transfer all markings, including notches and dots, from the muslin pieces to the slipcover fabric.

Sewing the Slipcover

Although the slipcover for your piece of furniture may be somewhat different from the style shown, many of the construction steps will be the same. It will be helpful for you to lay out the pieces and think through the sequence for sewing the seams of your slipcover. The labeled notches on adjoining seams will help you see how the pieces are to be joined together. To minimize the handling of bulky quantities of fabric, stitch any small details, such as darts, before assembling the large pieces.

For durable seams, use a strong thread, such as long-staple polyester, and a medium stitch length of about 10 stitches per inch (2.5 cm). Because slipcovers have several thicknesses of fabric at intersecting seams with welting, use a size 90/14 or 100/16 sewing machine needle.

Add welting to any seams that will be subjected to stress and wear, because welted seams are stronger than plain seams. For decorative detailing, welting can also be added to seams such as around the outside back and at the upper edge of the skirt. On furniture with front arm pieces, welting is usually applied around the front arm as a design detail. To prevent welted seams from puckering, take care not to stretch either the welting or the fabric as the seam is stitched. When a welted seam will be intersected by another seam, remove ½" (1.3 cm) of cording from the end of the welting to prevent bulk at the seamline.

For a chair, apply a zipper to one of the back seams of the slipcover. For a sofa, apply zippers to both back seams.

How to Sew a Slipcover with a Pleated Front Arm

1) Stitch darts at upper corners of inside back. If welting is desired, apply it to upper and front edges of outside arm, pivoting at corner.

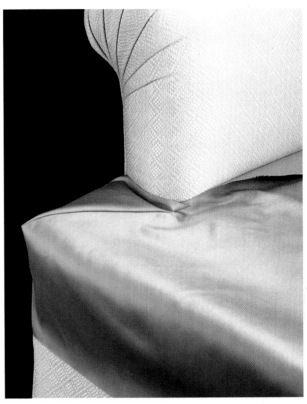

2) Stitch darts at outer front corners of deck; stop stitching ½" (1.3 cm) from raw edge at inner corner.

3) Stitch deck to front of arm and inside arm; this can be stitched as two separate seams.

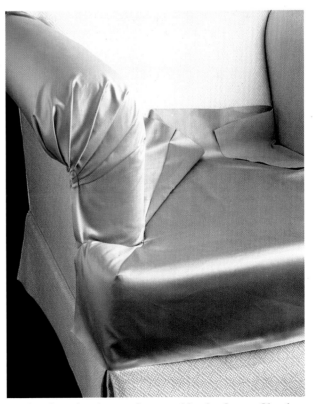

4) Pin pleats in place at front and back of arm. Check the fit over arm of chair. Baste in place on seamline.

(Continued on next page)

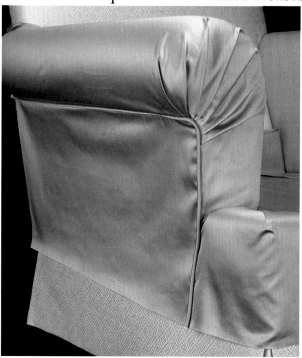

5) Stitch the horizontal and vertical seams, joining outside arm to inside arm; pivot at corner.

6) Pin inside arms to inside back on both sides **(a)**. Pin lower edge of inside back to back edge of deck **(b)**. Make tucks in seams at corners, if necessary, so pieces fit together. Stitch seams.

7) Apply welting around sides and upper edge of slipcover unit (page 65); curve ends of welting into seam allowance ½" (1.3 cm) from the lower edges (arrow). Join slipcover unit to outside back, leaving seam open for zipper application. Apply welting to lower edge.

8) Stitch skirt pieces together, leaving seam at back corner unstitched for zipper insertion; press seams open. Fold skirt in half lengthwise, wrong sides together; press.

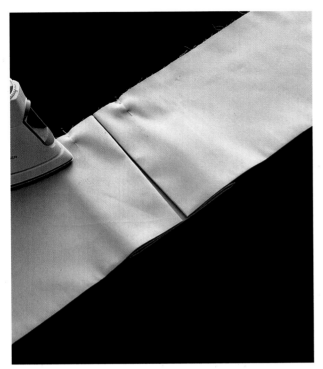

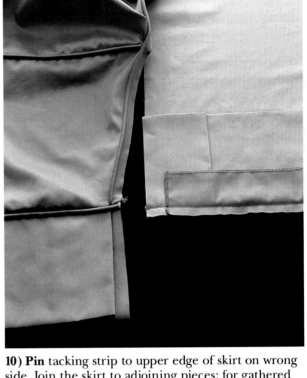

9) Press pleats for pleated skirt. Or for gathered skirt, stitch gathering stitches by zigzagging over a cord as on page 101, step 9; for skirt with bunched gathers, stitch gathering stitches between the markings.

10) Pin tacking strip to upper edge of skirt on wrong side. Join the skirt to adjoining pieces; for gathered skirt, pull up gathers to fit. Apply zipper (page 121). Sew cushions (pages 123 to 125).

11) Apply slipcover to furniture. Secure tacking strip to furniture by pinning into upholstery with T-pins.

12) Push extra fabric allowance into crevices around the deck and inside back. Stuff 2" (5 cm) strips of polyurethane foam into crevices around deck to keep fabric from pulling out. Insert cushions.

How to Sew a Slipcover with Front Arm Piece

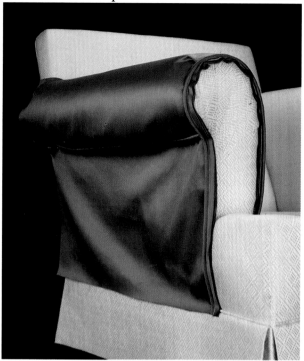

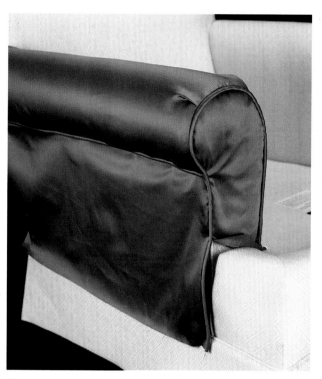

1) Stitch darts at upper corners of inside back. Apply welting to the upper edge of inside arm, if desired. Stitch horizontal seam, joining the outside arm to the inside arm. Pin and baste tucks at front edge of inside/outside arm. Apply welting to front edge of inside/outside arm.

2) Stitch the front arm piece to the front edge of inside/outside arm; stop stitching 2" (5 cm) from outer end of front arm piece.

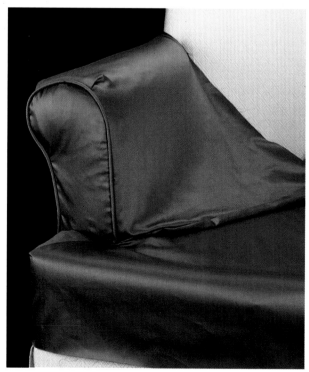

3) Follow steps 2 and 3 on page 117. Pin pleats in place at back of arm; baste in place on seamline.

4) Complete vertical seam at front edge of outside arm. Finish the slipcover as in steps 6 to 12 on pages 118 and 119.

How to Apply the Zipper

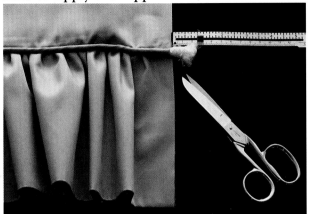

1) **Pull** the cording out slightly from ends of skirt opening; trim off ends 1" (2.5 cm). Pull seam to return cording to original position.

2) **Press** under seam allowances on zipper opening. Place open zipper on welted side of seam, so welting just covers zipper teeth and with zipper tab at lower edge. Pin in place; fold in seam allowance at lower edge of skirt to miter. Fold up end of zipper tape.

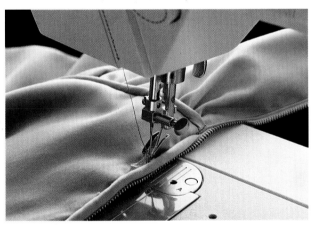

3) **Edgestitch** on skirt, using zipper foot, with zipper teeth positioned close to folded edge. Stitch in the ditch of the welted seam.

4) **Close** zipper. Place remaining side of zipper under seam allowance, with folded edge at welted seamline. Pin in place; fold in seam allowance at lower edge of skirt to miter. Fold up end of zipper tape.

5) **Open** zipper. Stitch ⅜" (1 cm) from folded edge, pivoting at top of zipper.

Pleated skirt. Follow steps 1 to 5, above, except break stitching at upper edge of the skirt. On skirt, stitch through lower layer of box pleat; stitch as close as possible to seam at upper edge of skirt.

Slipcovers for Cushions

You can make slipcovers for cushions on benches or window seats, as well as on sofas or chairs. Often cushions have welting at the edges, which adds strength to the seams. Plain welting (page 64) is most commonly used, but gathered welting (page 66) or twisted welting (page 68) may also be used.

To make it easier to insert the cushion, install a zipper across the back of the slipcover, extending around about 4" (10 cm) on each side. For cushions that are exposed on three sides, install a zipper across the back of the slipcover only. Use upholstery zippers, which are available in longer lengths than dressmaker zippers. The tab of the zipper will be concealed in a pocket at the end of the zipper opening. This is an upholsterer's technique that gives a professional finish.

✂ Cutting Directions

For a boxed cushion, cut the top and bottom pieces 1" (2.5 cm) larger than the cushion size to allow for seam allowances. T-cushions are pin-fitted, using muslin, to ensure accurate cutting. Cut two zipper strips, each the length of the zipper tape; the width of each zipper strip is equal to one-half the thickness of the cushion plus 1" (2.5 cm) for seam allowances. Cut a boxing strip the length of the cushion front plus twice the length of the cushion side; the width of the boxing strip is equal to the thickness of the cushion plus 1" (2.5 cm) for seam allowances. Seam strips together, as necessary. Cut welting strips for plain welting (page 64) or gathered welting (page 66).

YOU WILL NEED

Decorator fabric.

Zipper, about 8" (20.5 cm) longer than back edge of cushion.

Fabric and cording for fabric-covered welting; or twisted welting.

How to Cut the Fabric for a T-cushion

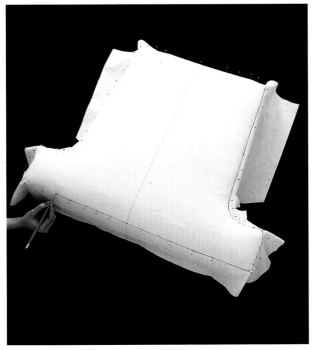

1) Cut muslin about 4" (10 cm) larger than top of cushion; mark grainline at center of fabric. Place muslin over cushion; pin along seamlines, smoothing out fabric. Mark seamlines along pin marks.

2) Remove muslin. True seamlines, using straightedge. Fold muslin in half to check that piece is symmetrical; make any necessary adjustments. Add ½" (1.3 cm) seam allowances. Cut cushion top and bottom from slipcover fabric. Cut zipper and boxing strips, opposite. Mark wrong side of fabric pieces, using chalk.

How to Sew a Slipcover for a Boxed Cushion

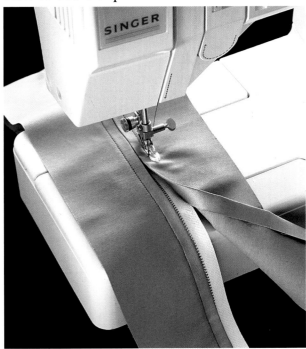

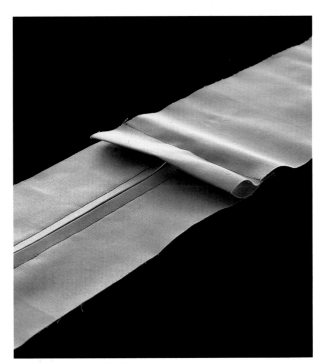

1) Press under ½" (1.3 cm) seam allowance on one long edge of each zipper strip. Position folded edges of strips along center of zipper teeth, right sides up. Using zipper foot, topstitch ⅜" (1 cm) from folds.

2) Press under 2" (5 cm) on one short end of the boxing strip. Lap the boxing strip over the zipper strip to cover zipper tab. Stitch through all layers 1½" (3.8 cm) from folded edge of boxing strip.

(Continued on next page)

3) Make and apply plain welting as on page 65, steps 1 to 5; gathered welting as on pages 66 and 67, steps 1 to 7; or twisted welting as on pages 68 and 69, steps 1 to 5. Stitch welting to right side of top and bottom pieces.

4) Place boxing strip on slipcover top, right sides together; center zipper on back edge. Start stitching 2" (5 cm) from zipper end, crowding cording. Clip corners as you come to them; stop stitching 4" (10 cm) from starting point.

5) Clip to mark seam allowances at ends of boxing strip. Stitch boxing strip ends together. Trim excess fabric; finger-press seam open. Finish stitching boxing strip to slipcover top.

6) Fold boxing strip, and clip seam allowance to mark lower corners; be sure all corners are aligned with corners on slipcover top. Open zipper.

7) Place boxing strip and slipcover bottom right sides together. Match clips of boxing strip to corners of slipcover bottom; stitch. Turn right side out.

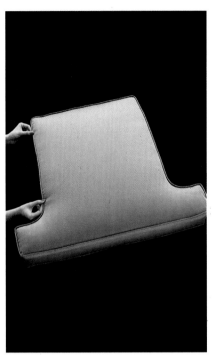

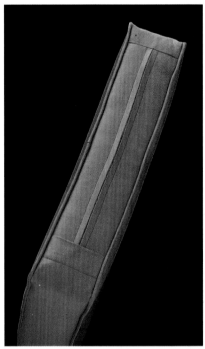

8) Fold cushion to insert it into slipcover. If necessary, wrap cushion with plastic to help slide it into slipcover; then remove plastic.

9) Stretch cover from front to back. Close zipper. Smooth cushion from center to edges. Stretch welting taut from corner to corner to square the cushion.

Alternative zipper placement. Install zipper across the back of slipcover, without extending it around the sides, if slipcover will be exposed on three sides.

How to Match a Patterned Fabric on a Boxed Cushion

1) Cut slipcover top and boxing strip so pattern matches at front seamlines. Notch front corners on upper and lower edges of boxing strip.

2) Stitch boxing strip to front edge of slipcover top first. Then continue stitching boxing strip to slipcover top and bottom.

Index

Cy DeCosse Incorporated offers
sewing accessories to subscribers.
For information write:
  Sewing Accessories
  5900 Green Oak Drive
  Minnetonka, MN 55343